STRAIGHT TO
THE TOP
AND BEYOND

*Adventure isn't hanging on a rope on the side of a mountain.
Adventure is an attitude that we must apply to the day-to-day
obstacles of life—facing new challenges, seizing new opportunities,
testing our resources against the unknown and, in the
process, discovering our own unique potential.*

STRAIGHT TO THE TOP AND BEYOND

Nine Keys for Meeting the Challenge of Changing Times

John Amatt

Johannesburg • London
San Diego • Sydney • Toronto

Composition and Scans: IBEX Graphic Communications Inc.

Cover Photograph: Bruno Engler

Interior Photographs: Bruno Engler, pp. xi, 62; Pat Morrow, pp. 57, 66, 68, 72, 76, 78, 81, 85, 103, 105, 110

Artwork: p. 60 - reprinted by permission of Air Canada; p. 91 - reprinted by permission of *The Edmonton Sun*; p. 119 - reprinted by permission of the National Maritime Museum, London, England

Published by Pfeiffer & Company
8517 Production Avenue
San Diego, CA 92121-2280
United States of America

Editorial Offices: (619) 578-5900; FAX (619) 578-2042
Orders: USA (606) 647-3030; FAX (606) 647-3034

Printed in the United States of America

Printing 1 2 3 4 5 6 7 8 9 10

Library of Congress Cataloging-in-Publication Data
Amatt, John.
    Straight to the top and beyond / John Amatt.
        p.   cm.
    ISBN 0-89384-296-6 (hard)
    1. Success—Psychological aspects. 2. Change (Psychology)
3. Adaptability (Psychology)   I. Title.
BF637. S8A47   1996
158'. 1—dc20   95-48869
                                      CIP

This book is printed on acid-free, recycled stock that meets or exceeds the minimum GPO and EPA specifications for recycled paper.

For my parents,
whose self-sacrifice, courage and
dedication to effort enabled me to explore
my own limits and discover the person
that I had become.

CONTENTS

Special Thanks

I am constantly amazed at how small, seemingly unrelated events—when added together over a period of time—can have a major impact upon the outcome of one's life. In writing this book, I have enjoyed looking back across many years of personal experience and have relived many events that had faded into the past. In reviewing these memories, one thing clearly stands out: it's people who make the difference. And, in my life, I've been associated with some pretty special people.

Pride of place goes to my parents, Syd and Dot Amatt, who provided the foundation of security from which I could launch myself into the unknown during those early years. As a youngster growing up in England, like many kids I tended to take my parents for granted. They were always there when I needed support. And they never tried to stop me from achieving my dreams, no matter how risk-filled or unpredictable they may have seemed. At the time, this meant little to me, but as a parent myself I realize now that this took tremendous courage and mental sacrifice. I can only hope they feel today that this personal investment of themselves in my future has paid off.

In recent years, a similar sacrifice has been made by my wife, Peggy, and my daughter Jillian, who have withstood my frequent absences and supported my dreams every step of the way. I think we have all grown through the experience.

Some years ago, Peggy led a group of friends on an adventure tour to Africa, where they planned to visit game parks and hike up Kilimanjaro, at 19,340 feet the highest mountain on that continent. Before leaving, she was inundated with advice from my well-meaning climbing friends, who insisted that she must undergo a rigorous training period if she were to have any hope of success. Knowing her limitations, however, she determined not to be pushed by others and to set her own slow pace on the mountain. At three o'clock one morning, I was woken from a deep sleep by a phone call from Peggy in Mombasa, Kenya, telling me she had gone all the way to the top. Surprisingly, it was only the second mountain she had tried to climb, the first being an eight-thousand-foot summit in the Canadian Rockies!

As I write, Jillian is in the midst of a ten-month educational odyssey with Class Afloat, sailing with forty-eight other students, teachers and crew aboard the *S/V Concordia*, a 188-foot tall ship, from Vancouver to Hawaii, the Marshall Islands, the Solomon Islands, northern Australia, Indonesia and across the Indian Ocean via Christmas Island, Cocos Islands, the Chagos and Seychelles to Mombasa on the African coast. After an inland game safari in Kenya, she will rejoin the ship in Cape Town, before sailing to Namibia, and across the Atlantic Ocean via St. Helena to Natal and Belem in Brazil, where the group will explore the Amazon River basin. Traveling northward through the Caribbean islands and the eastern seaboard of the United States, the Class Afloat brigade will finally reach Sydney, Nova Scotia, after having sailed around the world in three hundred days. Truly, she has developed an attitude for adventure, and I know she will continue to seek out exciting new challenges in her future.

Any success that I have achieved in my current career has been the result of a dedicated team of associates at One Step Beyond WorldWide—Mike Simpson, Lois Hunter, Janine Thrale, Tim Birnie, Al Justason, Marni Virtue; and our joint-venture colleagues from the Pacific Centre for

John, Jillian and Peggy Amatt—above our mountain town of Canmore in the Canadian Rockies.

Leadership—Barb Hertell, Christo Grayling, Lorne Armstrong and Mike Shaw. To them all, many thanks for hanging in over all these years.

And I would be remiss if I didn't acknowledge the contributions of the exceptional achievers who have worked with us in building the company, many of whom are quoted in the pages that follow:

Sharon Wood, first North American woman to climb Everest and just the sixth woman to achieve this amazing feat.

Laurie Skreslet, who became the first Canadian to reach the top of the world, when he reached the summit of Everest with our Canadian team in 1982.

Pat Morrow, another Everest colleague, who was the

second Canadian to reach the world's highest peak and the first person to climb the Seven Summits, reaching the highest point on each continent.

Carl Hiebert, confined to a wheelchair after a hang-gliding accident, but who now flies an ultralight aircraft and carries his Gift of Wings story to people nationwide.

Laurie Dexter, an Anglican minister from the Northwest Territories, who was a member of the joint Canadian-Russian team which, for the first time in history, skied across the frozen Arctic Ocean via the North Pole.

John Hughes, a solo around-the-world sailor, who lost his mast while sailing across the southern Pacific Ocean and jury-rigged a sail from spinnaker poles before continuing around Cape Horn through some of the roughest seas on the planet.

Mike Beedell, an Arctic explorer and photographer who, with Jeff MacInnis, became the first to cross the Northwest Passage using only wind power, sailing for more than three summers in an open catamaran.

Hundreds of thousands of people have been inspired by the gripping stories of these exceptional achievers and, through example, have learned to become more adventurous in their own lives.

Last, I must acknowledge a debt of gratitude to the dedicated professionals who were involved in the publication of this book—Alan Hobson of Calgary, who was commissioned by One Step Beyond WorldWide to write a biographical profile of my life from which this book has evolved; Erin Palmer of Canmore, whose preliminary draft helped me to focus my attention on the job of writing; Maggie Paquet of Vancouver, who subjected my original manuscript to her usual thorough edit; and Denise Schon and Nicole de Montbrun, publisher and editor at Macmillan Canada in Toronto, who shepherded the project through to completion.

To everyone who shares the Adventure Attitude, I trust that the efforts of all these exceptional people will continue to be an inspiration.

Personal success and happiness are largely a matter of what we do in our minds. The mind, and what we choose to put in it, determines greatness. It's not some arbitrary set of circumstances, fluke or chance that molds great people. Great people are the products of what is in their heads and hearts.

—*Alan Hobson*

MEETING THE CHALLENGE OF CHANGE

The art of progress is to preserve order amid change and to preserve change amid order.

—*Alfred North Whitehead*

THIS IS A BOOK ABOUT change and about how to meet the challenges of the coming millennium by continually striving to go one step beyond your previous experience. It is also a book about achievement in the face of uncertainty, and about learning the lessons from the daily struggles we all face. More than anything else, it is a book about discovering the potential that lies within and making the most of the opportunities that are offered to us throughout our lives.

We are living through one of the great transitional periods of human history, where economic, political and social changes are occurring with lightning speed. Events taking place on the opposite side of the earth inexorably influence our daily lives. We cannot stop change, nor can we ignore it. But we can increase our ability to adapt, to manage change effectively and to benefit from the adversity that change creates.

In these rapidly changing times, the metaphor of adventure offers the perfect vehicle for articulating a strategy that will help us address this challenge. By definition, an adventure is a journey with an uncertain outcome, and adventurers are people who actively seek out difficulty in order to stretch their potential against the unknown.

Today, the pace of change dictates that we must all become adventurers, leaving behind the known world of our previous experience and moving with confidence into the unpredictable world of the next millennium.

To succeed in the twenty-first century, we must learn to embrace change, to become comfortable with uncertainty and to become visionary and adventurous in dealing with the new social, political and economic environments in which we will, like it or not, be forced to live.

The challenge of change is forcing us to rethink our values and to rekindle the spirit of adventure. It will take courage, resourcefulness and endurance to meet this challenge—the courage to try, to commit and to take risks; the resourcefulness to be innovative and creative in finding new ways of doing old things; and the endurance to keep going when the going gets tough.

In meeting the challenge of change, one of the greatest difficulties will be in shaking off the suffocating demands for security that dominate the lives of so many people. Over the years, in seeking to support those in our society who are unable to look after themselves, we have created a wide-ranging security net that is resulting in an alarming trend toward individuals who no longer seem willing to take personal responsibility for the consequences of their own actions.

Increasingly, we see a growing component of society that looks toward government, the law courts or the insurance industry to bail them out when something goes wrong or when the going gets tough. And all of this is occurring at a staggering financial cost that we can no longer afford.

But this was not originally the case! The world we take so much for granted today is a society that has evolved through centuries of risk-taking by our predecessors, for whom every day was an adventure. The explorers, fur traders, settlers and pioneers who developed this land had no security system on which to fall back. These were people who saw the opportunities offered by this vast continent and had the courage to let go of security in accepting the risks the new world would demand. And they were also willing to accept the consequences of their actions, whether the results were positive or negative. It would never have occurred to them that life could be led in any other way.

It is one of the great paradoxes of human existence that, by nature, we seek out comfort and predictability, using all of our financial resources and intellectual powers to devise technologies that will make our lives easier and less stressful. The paradox is that once we have created the comfort we desire, we must leave it all behind if we are to move forward toward future opportunity.

The problem of security, of course, is that once attained, it becomes increasingly difficult to let go. To progress as a society, we have to leave behind our established comfort zones and leap one step beyond into the future. Such a step demands courage and commitment, but once taken, will lead to increasing excitement and opportunity. All kinds of things will start to occur that would never have resulted if that initial step had not been taken.

In fact, the adventure of life is only to be found by continually striving to go one step beyond in search of discovery and new challenge. Children do this as a matter of course, but, as adults, we must force ourselves never to be satisfied with the secure world we have created through our past efforts. Instead, we should continually be placing ourselves out on a limb, where we have to perform to our maximum potential. In adopting this philosophy, we will have to take risks, but risks that have been carefully controlled through adequate preparation and analysis—and risks for which the resulting consequences have been carefully considered, acknowledged and personally accepted.

In the process, we will discover our real selves—and gain a better understanding of our real potential. We owe it to ourselves to continue to search for a more complete awareness of the strengths we can apply to our goals in life, and also for a more pragmatic and realistic acceptance of the limitations we carry within us. After all, it is our strengths *and* our limitations that make us who we are—and without full knowledge of both, we can never be fully aware of what we are capable of achieving with our lives.

The trick is to set increasingly difficult goals as we progress through life. Having attained each goal in turn—and increased our knowledge of our own potential in the process—we can gaze off into the metaphorical distance and project what the future might bring. But, as we come down off each peak of achievement, we must continually apply this new-found knowledge of self toward even higher peaks, as we struggle forward toward the next horizon of endeavour.

There are places to go beyond belief.

—*Neil Armstrong*

ONE

TAKING THE FIRST STEPS

Security is mostly a superstition. It does not exist in nature, nor do the children of man as a whole experience it. Avoiding danger is no safer in the long run than outright exposure. Life is either a daring adventure, or nothing!

—*Helen Keller*

ADVENTURERS ARE MADE, not born. They are the products of their lifetime experiences and their belief that, in the final analysis, they alone are ultimately accountable for the consequences of their actions.

Certainly, my unremarkable beginnings near Manchester, in the heart of industrial Britain, betrayed no hint of the adventurous exploits to come. My family was traditional and conservative. My father, Sydney, was a senior bank official who went to work every day wearing a pin-stripe suit and carrying a black umbrella. The day he retired after thirty-eight years with the same bank, he jumped on his bowler hat and never looked back. My mother, Dorothy, was a full-time homemaker who was always there to look after me. I lived in a protected environment where it was not necessary for me to take any risks. As a result, I lacked self-confidence and was painfully shy.

One of my earliest memories is of a family holiday in southern England when I was about eight years old. We had been driving in the family car and had become lost. It was starting to become dark. As we came to a row of houses in a small village, my father asked me to get out of the car and ask someone for directions to the hotel. I was stricken with panic. Tears welled up in my eyes. With head down and arms folded tightly across my chest, I refused to leave the car. The idea of speaking to a stranger was something I simply could not face.

Some thirty years later, I walked across the stage of Radio City Music Hall in New York City, the largest indoor theater in the world, to address six thousand people at the fifty-seventh annual meeting of the Million Dollar Round Table, a prestigious international life insurance organization. I was there to speak about my experiences as a member of the first Canadian expedition to reach the summit of Mount Everest.

How did I make the transition from that shy eight-year-old boy who could not speak to one stranger to a man who could stand on a stage and address six thousand? The answer lies in my experiences in the mountains, where, as a young man, I began to discover my true potential.

Mountains have always been very significant to me and have, in fact, shaped my entire personality. Once I began to climb as a teenager, I developed the confidence I had lacked as a child. The satisfaction and self-esteem I drew from mountaineering remained with me. As a result, my experiences in the mountains were translated into other areas of my life in ways I could never have imagined.

It was in my father's library that I had my first vicarious taste of adventure. Dad had grown up in the shadow of the great English explorers of the early twentieth century—men like Robert Falcon Scott, who had lost his life returning from the South Pole when my father was just a boy.

In their early years together, my parents had pursued their own adventures. On their honeymoon in 1936, they

My parents, Syd and Dot Amatt (second and third from right), pause outside the Gleckstein Hut during their climb of the Wetterhorn in 1938.

climbed in the Bernese Alps of Switzerland and, two years later, reached the summit of the 12,142-foot Wetterhorn, a mountain my sister and I would also climb when I was eighteen years old. Also in 1938, they were present in Grindlewald when the deadly north face of the Eiger was climbed for the first time, at that point, the most dramatic climb in history. So even though my father was not actively involved in mountaineering, he was keenly interested in it. Over the years, he amassed a considerable collection of books and articles about Himalayan climbing and other adventures, including *The White Spider*, the history of the Eiger north face, and books chronicling early attempts on Everest. And it was there, with my nose buried in leather-bound books and yellowed press clippings, that I first dreamed of standing on unconquered summits.

I made my first mountain conquest, somewhat reluctantly, at the age of eleven. That year, on a holiday in Scotland, I set out with my parents and my older sister, Susan, on a day hike up Ben Nevis, at 4,406 feet the highest mountain in the British Isles. It was a long trek to the summit and halfway up the weather turned cold, the wind driving rain into our faces. Predictably, I became tired, bored and extremely uncomfortable. Soon I was grumbling about wanting to go back to the car.

I will never forget my father standing before me and staring down with a stern face. "If you turn around now," he said, "you'll regret it for the rest of your life."

His words hit home and I felt the heat of anger rising up inside me. I'd show him, I thought. I pulled my jacket tight against the freezing rain and doggedly pushed on up the trail with my sister. My parents soon fell behind, anxiously asking other

On top of Ben Nevis—age eleven years—with my mother and sister.

hikers if they had seen two youngsters up ahead. When they finally reached the top, Susan and I had been there for an hour, shivering in the icy cold.

There is a lesson to be learned in everything we do, but we must set our minds to seeking out the learning and not let these opportunities pass us by.

At the time, that event meant nothing to me. Yet it was undoubtedly a transitional point in my life. In fact, it was probably the catalyst that produced the person I am today. Because if I had not been challenged to keep going, I would probably not have continued to follow the path into mountaineering. But those few words from my father turned me right around.

The real changes in my personality began that fall, when I transferred to Bolton School, a British public school that boasted a very active outdoor program. There I also joined the school's scout troop and, on weekend camping and hiking trips, began to discover the thrill of the unknown. Gradually, I acquired self-confidence and a sense of independence I never knew I had. I began to reach a little further for my dreams and to discover that it was effort that produced the desired results.

When I joined the scouts, my father pointed out that there were a number of badges I could easily earn. But I told him, "I'm not interested in that, Dad. When I put a badge on this arm, I want it to mean something." In order to really appreciate the award, I felt that I had to work to achieve it.

In order to earn a scouting badge when I was fourteen, I set my sights on building a scale model of the bridge on the River Kwai, which I had seen in the then-recent hit movie. But I needed an accurate picture of the bridge from which to create my model. After many inquiries, my father located the firm in Sheffield that had developed the original plans for the bridge. He wrote to them and got a copy of the blueprints.

The bridge on the River Kwai.

When completed, my bridge was more than five feet long, constructed out of thousands of pieces of dowel individually cut to length and precisely fitted into position. There was not a single nail in the entire structure–the pieces were painstakingly lashed together with cord. It took three months to build, and I wanted to quit hundreds of times. But my father would not let me. He kept pushing me to finish it. His constant encouragement taught me that if something is worth starting, it is also worth finishing. After it was completed, I donated it to my scout troop, where it remains on display to this day.

As I approached mid-teens, my father and I began to undertake multi-day backpacking trips together, several of them requiring long journeys into northern Scotland. After a full day of driving from our house outside Manchester, we would pitch a tent beside the car on the edge of some remote moorland. Following an early morning breakfast of bacon and eggs, we would shoulder our packs and head for the hills. On one memorable occasion, we spent three days traversing the famous Llarig Gru, a twenty-seven-mile circuit that bisects the rugged Cairngorm Mountains near Aviemore in central Scotland.

At the same time, I was developing a love for the natural world. From an early age, I had been interested in bird-watching, and many weekends would find us lying behind a blind next to a remote lake or marsh, peering through binoculars to identify rare species of migrating birds as they arrived from places unknown. As I grew older, I started to breed butterflies and moths in specially built cages in a shed at the back of our house. Rushing home from school in the late afternoon, my task would be to cut leaves from suitable trees to feed my growing collection of voracious caterpillars. Weeks later, they would transform into dormant cocoons and, the following spring, appear in brilliant colors, their fragile wings spreading before my curious eyes.

For the most part, however, those early years remain gray in my memory. It was not until my sixteenth year—the year I began climbing—that things came into clearer focus. After returning from a trip to Austria with my family, I announced that I wanted to start rock climbing. Having seen a group of adventurers hanging from ropes on a roadside crag, I was fired by excitement.

Before long, I had contacted the Lancashire Caving and Climbing Club, which held weekly meetings in a dingy room above a pub in Bolton. I can still recall walking around the block several times before I could summon up the courage to go inside to introduce myself. But joining the climbing club was to be a breakthrough experience. From this point onward, I could join club members for weekends climbing in North Wales or the English Lake District, often staying in the club hut below Dow Crag near Coniston.

Despite their concerns for my safety, my parents always supported and encouraged me in my climbing activities. In fact, they went out of their way to help. Today, as a parent myself, I have great appreciation for the courage they displayed in letting me go my own way, not knowing whether I was safe, but putting their faith in my ability to return home again after each weekend foray into the unknown.

The first time my father and I really climbed together was on Tryfan in North Wales. This was the mountain where the British Everest expedition had tested its oxygen system before putting Edmund Hillary and Tenzing Norgay on top of the world in 1953. I recall that we set out for the summit of Tryfan with a piece of nylon rope that was not actually a climbing rope at all; it was a washing line that I had picked up cheaply at a local hardware store. Dad wanted to climb to the peak by the easiest route. But I was looking for a challenge. I told him, "You don't understand, Dad. You've got to do the difficult bits." Again, it was the effort that counted.

At that time, climbing was so popular in England that the British Broadcasting Corporation regularly aired live telecasts of rock climbing from the nearby gritstone outcrops of Derbyshire and Yorkshire. One legendary climber featured in these programs was Joe Brown, whose nickname was The Human Fly. He was a plumber by trade, but he had made the first ascent of Kangchenjunga, the world's third highest mountain. He was so well known that fans could simply address their letters to "Joe Brown, Human Fly, England" and the post office would locate him.

When I was not out climbing myself, I would be glued to the television watching my hero climb. The suspense was incredible. Since the broadcast was live, everyone knew he could fall off at any moment, given the extreme nature of the climbs he was attempting.

After one such broadcast, I commented to my father, "Boy, I'd love to climb with Joe Brown." Within days, Joe called me on the telephone.

Understandably, my parents were becoming concerned for my safety as I began to tackle more and more difficult routes, so my father took the trouble to set up a training session with Joe Brown to ensure I was using the proper precautions. But climbing with Joe also inspired me to greater heights. It was like climbing with the greatest hero you could ever imagine—like a young kid playing hockey with Wayne Gretzky. The first time I climbed with him, I climbed three grades of difficulty higher than I ever had before.

Despite the difference in our ages (Joe was in his mid-thirties, I in my late teens), we were to become good friends, and he introduced me to a whole new level of the sport. Through Joe I met other members of Britain's climbing elite, including Chris Bonington, who would become the renowned leader of many expeditions to Mount Everest. The

Joe Brown (top) and John Amatt climbing in England.

days I spent with Joe Brown had a significant effect on my personality and opened up many doors to future opportunities in the sport.

From the beginning, the thrill of climbing for me was the process of seeing a rock face that you thought you could never climb, but trying it and finding out that you could. I was learning that the perception of an untried reality is always much worse than the reality itself. Through climbing, I was discovering that if you took a problem one step at a time and worked out the sequence of moves, you could make the seemingly impossible become possible. Every weekend, I was testing my mental and physical resources, my strengths and my limitations against increasingly difficult objectives. And in the process, I was becoming a more fulfilled and effective person.

In an early article that I wrote for a climbing magazine, I noted, "Climbers always feel some element of fear on a climb. Success lies in testing your mental resources in overcoming this fear. It is this success that will ultimately lead to what might be called courage. For courage is not an innate quality, but one that is developed by facing up to premeditated danger and overcoming it."

While I was in Bolton School, I struggled academically for some time and, as a result, had to repeat my fifth year. At the time, this was a somewhat disappointing experience, but in retrospect was probably the best thing that could have happened. It taught me once again that we only really appreciate the things in life that we have had to struggle to achieve.

But in climbing, I had found something I was good at, and, for the first time, I started to get recognition from my peers. I began to develop the confidence to go farther afield. I was never satisfied. I was always trying to be better, to climb harder and harder—and in the process I was discovering more and more about myself. I wanted to experience the thrill of discovery, the exploration of unclimbed peaks and of my own potential.

In my final year at Bolton School, I took advantage of a recently established school trust fund to organize a four-man expedition to a remote region of northern Norway. Crossing the North Sea during some of the worst storms in recent memory, we traveled northward for five days, journeying by coastal ferry from Bergen to the small town of Narvik, close to the Lofoten Islands and inside the Arctic Circle. Establishing our base camp in remote Skjomen Valley, we made six first ascents on unclimbed peaks in the Storsteinsfjell Massif over a three-week period. Our equipment was unsophisticated, to say the least: construction hats for helmets and bare rope tied directly around our waists. (Modern climbing harnesses had yet to be invented.)

　　　This expedition was my first real departure from the beaten path, and it pointed the way for me into the future. Up until that point, I had visited Switzerland and Italy and hiked on trails where millions of other people had hiked previously. But it was not until our visit to Arctic Norway that I climbed where no one had been before. From that point onward, everything I did I tried to do in remote areas that few had visited. It was here that I discovered there is no greater thrill than stepping out from the crowd, going where no foot has trodden previously. It was exciting to be challenging the unknown and to be first.

　　　When I got back from that expedition, I joined a group of local climbers who had also just returned from northern Norway. On their way home, they had visited the Romsdal Valley in central Norway, where they had been told of a sheer mountain face called the Troll Wall, the Wall of the Giants in local mythology. It was reportedly vertical, smooth and hold-less for five thousand feet. We had heard stories of climbers who had dropped stones from the summit and watched them fall all the way to the valley floor without ever touching the cliff. It was the highest vertical mountain precipice in the world, a vertical mile. Nobody had ever climbed it. In fact, some of the world's best climbers had said it was impossible.

　　　In 1965, at the age of twenty and fired by the idealism and ambition of youth, Bill Tweedale, Tony Nicholls, Tony

Howard and I teamed up to attempt the first ascent of the Troll Wall. It was a huge step into the unknown on our part, mixed with a certain degree of ignorance. The highest vertical face I had climbed in Britain at that point was about three hundred feet. Yet now I was proposing to inch my body five thousand feet above the ground on a smooth rock face that expert climbers had deemed impossible. We were the first to even attempt it. If something went wrong up there, we knew no one would be able to help us and we would probably die.

The essence of adventure is being willing to step out into an experience that you don't totally understand. The essence of achievement is exploring that unknown.
—*Laurie Dexter*

TWO

THE VERTICAL MILE

*Until one is committed, there is hesitancy, the chance to draw back,
always ineffectiveness. Concerning all acts of initiative (and creation),
there is one elementary truth, the ignorance of which kills countless
ideas and splendid plans: that the moment one definitely commits one-
self, then Providence moves, too. All sorts of things occur to help one
that would never otherwise have occurred. A whole stream of events
issues from the decision, raising in one's favour all manner of unfore-
seen incidents and meetings and material assistance, which nobody
could have dreamt would have come their way. I have learned a deep
respect for Goethe's couplet:*

Whatever you can do, or dream you can, begin it.
Boldness has genius, power, and magic in it.

—W.H. Murray

WE ARRIVED IN THE
Romsdal Valley, four hundred miles north of Oslo, on July 1,
1965. As we set up camp, the entire valley was filled with cloud,
the surrounding peaks invisible to our curious gaze. Finally, after
four days of rain and fog, the mist began to clear and we caught
glimpses of jagged rock pinnacles disappearing straight up into
the sky. These were the Trolls, the mythical Norwegian giants
that defended the upper reaches of the face and gave the
mountain its name.

The next day the weather began to clear and we could, for the first time, see the full extent of what we had come to climb. It was not only vertical, but overhanging almost from top to bottom. As it neared the summit, the cliff flared out for more than one hundred feet, like the prow of a huge Viking ship.

In retrospect, I realize the hardest part of this climb, after all our planning and preparation and dreaming, was actually getting started. The night before, we had lain in our camp, trying to sleep, gazing up at that great black precipice and knowing that the next day we would be coming face-to-face with the unknown. We had established our advance camp on the scree at the base of the cliff. As we tried to sleep, avalanches thundered from the summit gullies above, and huge boulders crashed down through the mist.

A mixture of great apprehension and tremendous excitement infused the night. Turning restlessly in our sleeping bags, we wondered what it was going to be like up there on the wall; at the same time, we worried about everything that could go wrong. We knew that unless we got started first thing the next day, we would never discover if we were up to the challenge. That is the time when you are most tempted to turn around and go home. But you know if you do, you will never find out what you might have accomplished. Your pride says you've got to try, and so you do.

Looking back today, I realize that our attempt to make the first ascent of the Troll Wall was a huge leap of faith for us all. We probably did not fully appreciate the risks we were taking. At that time in Norway, there were no mountain rescue teams. If we had become stuck halfway up the face, there was absolutely nobody around who could have reached us. It was a real adventure, an exploration. It was going where nobody had gone before.

My father had asked me before we went to Norway how I could possibly think of climbing something that the experts had said was impossible. My answer was, "Well, if we can climb 150 feet the first day and another 150 feet the second

The five-thousand-foot vertical Troll Wall in Norway.

day, then we'll have gone 300 feet. Another 300 on top of that and we'll have done 600 feet. If we just keep doing that, we'll eventually climb a mile." By taking it one step at a time, the impossible could become possible.

When forced to confront fear, a lot of people step back. But those who step forward will move forward.

And so we forced the fear to the backs of our minds and began to inch our way up the cliff. By nightfall we had reached a small cave a hundred feet up the wall, with just enough room for the four of us to squat in our down jackets and sleeping bags. Tying ourselves to metal pegs driven into the rock, we settled down with our backs hard against the cliff, our heels dangling over the drop.

The next day, we climbed for sixteen hours straight, gaining five hundred feet of new ground through the maze of overhangs and grooves. Often the surface was too smooth to allow purchase and we had to drive metal pegs into the rock. At one point it took us more than an hour to gain only three feet. But by late that night, we had reached a tiny snow ledge, where we rested below a foreboding sweep of smooth granite we dubbed the Great Wall.

When we awoke next morning, the sky was clear but the wind had changed direction, driving storm clouds toward us from the sea. As the black clouds boiled out of the valley, the temperature dropped and the winds picked up. A light rain began to fall.

Despite the weather, we pressed on up the smooth face of the Great Wall, listening to the rocks whistling by behind us as they fell through the clouds from the overhangs above.

Again the climbing was painfully slow. As lead climber, I would inch my way up, standing in foot loops anchored to the rock by metal pegs. Balancing with a foot in one of the loops, I would drive a peg into the rock above my head and then attach the other foot loop to the higher anchor. Stepping up,

I would repeat the process and could thus laboriously cover long stretches of smooth terrain.

By midnight in the twilight of the northern sky, we had gained just 250 feet above our previous bivouac as Tony climbed up to join me on a tiny foothold right on the very edge of a thousand-foot sheer drop. We were only eighty feet from the top of the Great Wall, but a blank section blocked our progress.

By now the weather had closed in on us completely. The wind was gusting and driving torrents of freezing rain at the rock face. After twenty-three hours of climbing, we were exhausted. We could not possibly spend the night exposed to the storm in this position. Dejectedly, we realized there was only one thing to do—retreat to the snow ledge that we had passed hours before at the beginning of this difficult section.

It took all my courage to descend. Earlier in the day, I had been standing on a spike of rock when it suddenly broke off and I found myself hanging on the rope some fifteen feet below. With that memory still fresh in my mind, my body trembled as I fought to conquer my fear, my nose pressed to the cliff face, my hands gripping the anchor driven into the crack above my head.

Beside me, Tony Howard, the most experienced of the group, took control of the situation. Before I realized what was happening, he had disappeared into the void, calling for me to follow. I took hold of the rope, sucked in a deep breath and slipped over the edge. One hundred feet down the wall, exhaustion overcame me as I fell asleep, hanging by my climbing harness from a peg driven into the rock. Tony shook me awake and urged us all on as he struggled to bring us to shelter. Four hours later, our bodies shivering violently, we crawled onto the snow ledge and safety. Within minutes the full force of the storm struck.

As the storm grew in intensity, the four of us lay sandwiched in our nylon bivouac tents above the void. Inside, we snuggled in our wet clothes, drawing warmth from our companionship. No one spoke. Each was occupied with his own thoughts and fears. In the gloomy world of mist and dripping rock outside, the rain turned to sleet and drifted down, forming wet heaps in the hollows of our sacks. Before long we were lying in cold, wet puddles that quickly froze into solid ice.

Occasionally, we managed to scrape snow from the ground outside and melt it over the stove for a warm drink. Then we closed the flaps of our bags and lay inside, listening to the sleet splashing over our heads. I lay dozing in my sack with only the smallest of openings for air. Inside, the condensation of my breath trickled into my down jacket. Soon I was soaked to the skin and my outer clothing became stiff as armor as it began to freeze. We each suffered silently in our frozen cocoons, shivering violently through the two days and nights that the storm raged around us.

As dawn broke on the third day, the morning light barely penetrated the thick gloom of mist. The wind was still raging, and the sleet had turned to snow. Suffering from exposure and exhaustion, we lay there, too lethargic to move.

By now we were starting to get hypothermic. Because of the wet and cold, our bodies were losing heat rapidly. We knew that death could occur as our body temperatures dropped. In extreme conditions, the entire process can take as little as three hours. If we were to get down alive, we knew we had to leave now, while we still had the strength.

With great effort of will, we crawled out into the driving snow. Huddled against the wind, we forced our frozen fingers to sort gear and anchor the rope. Then, one by one, we lowered ourselves into the gloom, swinging down through plumes of water cascading from the wall above. For twelve desperate hours, we descended sheer rock that shimmered with newly formed ice.

As we progressed, the ropes became completely soaked and picked up grit from the rock. The gritty ropes cut into our soft, wet skin, and before long our hands were raw and bleeding. When we finally reached the foot of the wall, we staggered to the tent and collapsed into our sleeping bags in utter exhaustion.

It was the nearest we came to giving up.

For several days, we relaxed in the comfort of our valley camp while the storm continued to rage in the peaks far above. Then, refreshed by food, rest and dry clothes, we regrouped and decided to make another attempt. This time, the weather was with us, clear and dry. Once again, we returned to our assault camp and tried to sleep for a few hours at the base of the wall.

That night we lay in the dark, again confronting our fears. The silence was unbearable, broken only by the restless movements of my comrades and the occasional clatter of rock

Retreating from the Troll Wall in the storm (Tony Nicholls, Bill Tweedale and Tony Howard).

down the forbidding face nearby. Second after second ticked slowly by, inexorably stretching into minutes, the minutes into long, long hours. I was beginning to wish I had never attempted this climb.

When you run away from fear, it grows in your mind; when you move toward fear and confront it directly, it recedes.

Suddenly, the silence was broken by a terrifying thunder. We scrambled into action, ripping open the door of the tent and looking up at the dark, unfriendly cliff. A huge boulder was plummeting toward us. Before we could even cry out, the rock rumbled past, just feet from our camp. We collapsed into the tent, our minds racing.

After thirty paralyzing minutes, Tony Howard again took the lead.

"We're getting out of this bloody bowling alley," he said. "One more strike like that and we're all dead."

So in the early morning light, we moved sluggishly up to the base of the wall. Tony Nicholls's hands had been so badly slashed by the gritty ropes on our descent that he was unable to join us on this second attempt. He wished us well, and we began our struggle with the Troll Wall once more.

Throughout that day, as we moved upward in clear weather, we could hear the whistle of stones as they fell five thousand feet from the top of the cliff. Twice I was hit by stones the size of softballs dislodged by the lead climber. Bill Tweedale was hit in the kidneys by a falling rock, which doubled him over in pain.

As we climbed, we were able to shout across the face to a nearby group of fellow climbers. By coincidence, a Norwegian party had arrived to attempt to climb the Troll Wall by a different route, and the media were pitting us in a race for the top. Television cameras were taking pictures from across the valley, and helicopters buzzed around us. But competition was the farthest thing from our minds. As far as we climbers were concerned, we were all in this together. It was good to know we were not alone.

Moving more quickly because of our knowledge of the route, after nine hours of effort we once again reached the foot of the Great Wall. Since it was only just after noon, we decided to continue. Clawing my way up the featureless face, I scraped my knuckles raw as my grasping hands sought small fissures in the rock. My feet were held against the granite by pure friction.

By eleven that night, in the fading northern light, we had once again reached the small, wet overhang that had been our stumbling block on the first attempt. Suspending myself in my harness, I watched while Tony struggled to manoeuver up the bare section of rock.

Three hours later, I still had not moved. Tony had gained only thirty feet. "God damn it!" he yelled, "God damn this thing."

We were facing a big psychological barrier because this was the very point where we had been forced to abandon the first attempt in the storm only days before. We knew there were likely to be some ledges at the top of this blank section. But by now it was two o'clock in the morning and we found ourselves in the darkness standing on tiny footholds no wider than a boot. Reluctant to descend again, we decided to wait until morning.

In total, we had already spent more than thirty hours trying to overcome the three-hundred-foot vertical face of the Great Wall. We had no bivouac sacks to protect us and we were shaken endlessly by uncontrollable bouts of shivering. Tired, thirsty and hungry, I sucked water off the rock with my parched lips and nibbled at a fruit bar, chewing it slowly. I had only one foothold and had to alternate feet all night long. My friends dangled in harnesses above and below me. To make matters worse, a constant stream of water drained from the overhangs above. Before long, my clothing was soaked through once again.

Occasionally, I would drift off to sleep. Immediately, the leg that was supporting me would give way and I would jerk awake, hanging on the rope. It was lonely and quiet, each of us drifting with our thoughts, trying not to disturb the others in case they were managing to sleep. The only sign of life was the occasional jangle of climbing equipment or the slight tug on the rope as someone rubbed his cold hands or stretched his cramped muscles. We were waiting for the sun to revive us.

Despite the discomfort, I must have managed some rest, because I woke to feel the warmth of the sun on my face. From above, Tony called down in a raspy voice.

"Are you awake, John?"

I could only grunt in reply.

"Think I'll have another try," he said.

John Amatt leading on the Troll Wall.

And so at five o'clock, I watched as Tony started struggling up the wall again. I could hear him grunting with effort as he sought the tiny handholds, tapping metal pegs into blind cracks and breaking off fragments of rock that tumbled into the void below. The waiting was interminable and, tired from the short night, I began to nod off again.

Three hours later, I was jerked awake by his shouts from above.

"There's a fantastic ledge up here!" he cried. "Come on up."

We had finally overcome the Great Wall!

With a rush of adrenaline, Bill and I hauled ourselves up the rope to the ledge where Tony waited. After our grueling ordeal, we saw our dream come true: a five-foot-square grassy platform with a spring of water trickling down the rock. We lit the stove and heated up a meal of steak, vegetables and soup. Endless cups of tea were consumed. That night, perched in our throne room beneath the stars, we slept like kings.

The following morning we awoke fully rested. But because the summit was still a good three thousand feet above us, we were quickly on our way. The higher we got on the face, the more overhung and undercut it became. We were being forced farther and farther out over the void with nothing but thousands of feet of thin air beneath our heels.

The first couple of days we had really noticed that drop because our minds were more attuned to the horizontal world of the valley. But by the third day, we were becoming almost comfortable in this vertical world. As the days passed, we found ourselves throwing rocks and watching them fall into the nothingness below. Then we began to notice minute things like tiny flowers growing out of cracks and wondering how the seeds had lodged there. We began to realize the incredible powers of adaptation that lie within the human mind. If we can only move forward with optimism, overcome our natural fear of the unknown and embrace uncertainty, there is no adversity on earth that the human race cannot overcome.

Three days later, we were within sight of the top of the Troll Wall. We had climbed through a line of wet rock chimneys that cut through the final barrier of overhangs. And I had struggled to conquer my fear of being isolated in this desolate place.

That day, Tony had been leading and I had been climbing last. As he approached the overhanging section, he disappeared from view into the dark recesses of the chimney, his slow progress signaled by the jerking of the rope as it passed through Bill's hands. When it came tight, Bill had followed, leaving me alone on a tiny ledge. The only link to my companions was the rope snaking in space above my head.

For two hours, I waited for the rope to pull tight, indicating that I should start climbing. But it did not move. Tony and Bill were out of sight above the overhangs and I could not communicate with them. Isolated, my mind started to conjure all kinds of worst-case scenarios. Had they reached a blank section? Were they in trouble? Would we be forced to retreat from so high on the wall? Could we, in fact, get down? Because of the overhangs we had climbed through, our ropes were swinging in thin air beneath my feet, not even touching the rock.

A noise from above woke me from my reverie. The rope was moving and came tight. With immense relief, I started to climb and soon put the final barrier behind me. I had never before known such apprehension. I have never since experienced such an incredible feeling of isolation and helplessness than that I struggled to overcome that day alone on the Troll Wall.

Early the next morning, I led the final stretch to the summit. After being so long in the shadow of the north face, the thing we were most looking forward to was getting into the sun. As we looked up we could see it shining off the Trolls. With one final effort, I pulled myself over the top.

The morning sun streamed onto my face. I stretched my body, enjoying the freedom of movement, of being able to walk about without having to use my hands for balance. I stood for a moment, drinking in the magnificent view of the Romsdal Valley spread below, with the water of the nearby fjord shining green in the distance. Then I helped Tony and Bill over the final overhang and we hugged and cheered. As a signal to our friends in the valley, we spread a red bivouac sheet over the edge and watched the excitement erupt far below in base camp.

Suddenly, we were completely exhausted. It took half an hour just to walk the hundred-foot trail to the actual summit because we were so weak. We found it difficult to keep our balance because it had been ten days since we had been on level ground.

For three hours, we dozed in the sun. After so long in the shadow of the Trolls, our greatest pleasure was to lie there, our soaked clothes steaming in the heat. Finally, almost reluctantly, we shouldered our packs and started to hike down the gentle slopes at the back of the mountain. We had spent ten days climbing the vertical mile and it took only three hours to return to the valley. Along the way, a group of Norwegian climbers met us with beer. It went straight to our heads and, somewhat blissfully, we meandered our way into the waiting arms of our friends.

In the valley that night, I gazed again at the once fierce wall. Strangely, it now seemed almost friendly. We had explored its defenses and proved ourselves equal to the task. We had proved that the impossible was indeed possible. And we knew that we could never be the same people again.

We should never allow ourselves to be completely satisfied with our achievements in life. Because once we become satisfied, complacency will set in, and we will start to repeat things we have done before.

THREE

TOWARD THE NEXT HORIZON

Experience is not what happens to you. Experience is what you do with what happens to you.

—*Aldous Huxley*

OUR ASCENT OF THE Troll Wall shook the British climbing community and made the front pages of international climbing magazines. The Norwegian team had abandoned their original attempt to make a direct ascent of the Troll Wall and had opted instead for the east pillar. We had unquestionably made the first ascent of the vertical mile. Chris Bonington told me he thought it was the most important achievement by British climbers in a decade.

Success on the Troll Wall gave me my first taste of real achievement and it was another pivotal experience. With two friends, I had made the first ascent of the highest vertical mountain precipice in the world. In the weeks that followed, I began to think about what I had done. I started to realize that if I could do that, I could do anything. I also realized that if we had turned our backs at the bottom, we would never have learned that lesson. Climbing the Troll Wall showed me for the first time that if I could just make a start, take it one step at a time and remain committed to my goals despite all the setbacks, nothing is impossible. From there it became what's next, what's bigger, what's better, how do I grow?

Shortly after returning from Norway that fall, I was invited to join an important expedition that was being organized to explore the Cordillera Blanca region of South America the following summer. The expedition was being coordinated by Dennis Gray and Chris Bonington to give young, upcoming British climbers some high-altitude mountaineering experience. I had been recommended by Joe Brown and was invited on the strength of the Troll Wall climb.

We were going to climb the north ridge of Alpamayo, a twenty-thousand-foot peak in the Andes Mountains of Peru. The Swiss team, which first attempted to climb the mountain in 1948, declared it "the most beautiful mountain in the world," an assessment that has since been upheld by mountaineers the world over. A perfect trapezoid of fluted ice, Alpamayo is incredibly steep and seemingly impregnable from all angles. Although it had twice been attempted prior to our expedition, the main summit had never been reached by way of the complete north ridge.

At twenty-one years of age, I was very much the rookie on this expedition, but I recognized my inexperience and willingly accepted a secondary role, committing myself to carrying heavy loads of equipment in support of the more experienced climbers. I was excited just to be part of the team. It was my first major international expedition and my introduction to high-altitude climbing. I was also looking forward to learning more about filmmaking, as the expedition had been partially financed by a television station in Wales, which under the direction of Ned Kelly, a respected film and television producer, was making a film of the ascent.

Early in the climb, we had to negotiate a complex icefall, a mass of moving ice formed as the tumbling glacier descended over a rock ledge. In one place the route lay beneath an imposing ice cliff from which immense icicles hung like so many swords of Damocles. We called this section the Catwalk since we had to

Climbing in the Alpamayo Icefall.

tread warily across several fragile snow bridges above yawning crevasses as we dodged the hanging icicles with our heads.

To carry supplies to the camps on the upper mountain, we had to pass back and forth several times. It was always a dangerous spot and we would have stood little chance had one of the icicles fallen at the wrong time. That a crack appeared in the side of the cliff and was widening daily did not serve to boost our confidence. In fact, toward the end of the expedition, the cliff did collapse, burying our fixed ropes. Luckily no one was underneath, but the resulting traverse of the precariously balanced ice blocks called for steady nerves as we descended after the successful summit climb.

The other dangerous section was the Sugar Bowl, a huge depression where a series of ice pillars had collapsed into a wide crevasse, somewhat resembling sugar cubes piled into a glass bowl. To cross it, we had to thread our way delicately over numerous tenuous snow bridges spanning deep crevasses. This hollow in the glacier was a natural sun trap and the route became more treacherous each day as the bridges slowly melted away.

After three weeks of sustained effort, we had carried all of our equipment to our final camp at the foot of the north ridge and were at last in position to make the push to the summit. We were now higher than eighteen thousand feet, and the icy wind cut through our down jackets and outer clothing, making progress slow and uncomfortable.

We began by crossing a steep, featureless wall of ice. Beneath us, the slope dropped away in one smooth sweep to the glacier three-thousand feet below. Each hold had to be painstakingly carved into the ice. Slowly gaining height, we noticed how the strong winds had swept the snow into huge cornices, which curved out thirty feet over the drop. We had to move gingerly on the soft and unstable snow. In 1948, three members of the Swiss expedition had fallen more than six hundred feet from this same ridge when a similar cornice had snapped off under their weight. They were lucky to escape with their lives.

As we approached nineteen thousand feet, our lungs strained with the effort of breathing the thin air, and our muscles ached painfully with every step. We were only able to climb fifty feet at a time before having to stop for a few minutes of rest. Finally, step after plodding step, we found ourselves on the razor-edged summit ridge, balancing on our crampon points above the four-thousand-foot east face.

High on the north ridge of Alpamayo.

Climbing a vertical snow cone, we had to take turns standing on the actual summit because there was not enough room for two people to stand there together.

We were among only a handful of people to reach that spot and were rewarded with a view that stretched clear to the muted green of the Amazon basin, hundreds of miles to the east. In a later magazine story I commented, "We will never conquer majesty such as nature had laid out around us on that mountainside. But I learned in Peru that as long as we have eyes to see, we will keep trying."

I had broken a significant altitude barrier in my climbing career. But my experience on Alpamayo also taught me that successful expeditions do not rely on climbing ability alone. As the expedition equipment coordinator, I was in charge of finding manufacturers to donate gear. With youthful enthusiasm and ingenuity, I secured a full complement of state-of-the-art supplies by convincing sponsors that it was an honor to be invited to donate to our illustrious expedition.

In Peru, we were also tested by some unique logistical problems before the climbing could even begin, ranging from maniacal truck drivers to temperamental donkey caravans. At one point, we discovered that the bridge we had been assured would take us across a raging river had been washed out years before. We had to break open nine huge crates of equipment and ferry each item across on a swaying cableway.

These experiences taught me to be creative and flexible, to be willing and able to adapt quickly to unpredictable or new situations. It was these skills and the development of my promotional and organizational abilities that would contribute to my success on Mount Everest many years later.

On returning home from Peru that fall, I was hired by the British Broadcasting Corporation to work on a televised climb featuring Joe Brown, my hero from previous live telecasts. The program was to take place on Angelsey, an island off the coast of North Wales.

It was while staging this event that I met Rusty Baillie. With Dougal Haston, he had made the second British ascent of the north face of the Eiger. Rusty was quiet and philosophical, and impressed me with his determination to excel in all aspects of mountaineering. Having acknowledged my limitations as a young climber, I was looking for a more experienced partner to help push the limits of my ability, and Rusty and I hit it off perfectly. It was not long before we were climbing together in front of Scottish television cameras, making the first direct ascent of the Cobbler, a famous prow of rock that overhangs Loch Long north of Glasgow.

After climbing the Troll Wall, Alpamayo and the Cobbler, I had developed a reputation in climbing circles as something of a rising star. I was making money writing articles for magazines and giving lectures to climbing clubs. My fee was the princely sum of ten dollars for an evening's work!

But it was not long before I was looking for new challenges. Rusty had been very impressed by what we had done on the Troll Wall. So when I proposed going to try another

John Amatt climbing around the nose of the Cobbler. The ropes are hanging vertically!

unclimbed route in that same Norwegian valley, he jumped at the idea.

After the Troll Wall itself, the north face of Sondre Trolltind is the most impressive rock wall in the Romsdal Valley. After a 2,500-foot sweep of steepening approach slabs, it rises sheer and smooth for another 3,000 vertical feet. In many ways, it is even more challenging than the Troll Wall, for in all its height there is not a single ledge large enough to hold snow after a storm.

We have the ability to overcome every difficulty we face on earth. We have the ingenuity and intellectual power to find adaptive solutions to every situation. But we must use our minds to think and to question, and not complacently continue to operate by habit, doing things the way we have always done them.

In preparation for our attempt on Sondre Trolltind, we analyzed and refined every aspect of our strategy, questioned all the preconceived notions that we held in our minds and looked for improvements.

To combat the extreme wet conditions, we developed an innovative clothing system that included nylon-fiber sweaters originally designed for fishermen on the North Sea, waterproof sailing jackets and fingerless mitts. Each of these items has since become very popular among climbers.

We limited our provisions to peanuts and raisins, dried meat, boiled candies, rosehip syrup and chocolate so we could eat throughout the day as we climbed and not have to waste time cooking a meal. We warmed our water supply, so we would not waste valuable internal energy to bring its temperature up to that of our bodies after drinking.

We planned to sleep in hammocks nailed to the rock and to use innovative American climbing techniques and equipment, which had never before been used in Europe.

In so doing, we were launching a bare-bones effort, as there would only be the two of us climbing. We accepted that if anything went wrong, we could be in real trouble. But Rusty and I had the utmost faith and confidence in each other, having tested our friendship and trust on some of the most extreme climbs in the British Isles.

As we expected, the weather in Norway that summer was wet and inhospitable. For a week after our arrival, we rarely saw the mountaintops as rain swept through the valley.

The first clear morning, we rose with the crimson dawn and spent hours seeking out a route up the smooth, wet slabs to the upper wall. Climbing without ropes and carrying forty-pound sacks of gear on our backs, we felt very uncertain on the holdless slabs, where we were often relying solely on the friction of rubber soles on rock to stop a fall.

By mid-afternoon, we had arrived at the foot of the vertical upper wall. Here we became lost in the swirling mist and it became difficult to orient ourselves in relation to the route we had selected through binoculars from our valley. Cautiously, we decided to wait until the morning to continue.

Despite a forecast of bad weather, we awoke the following morning to clear skies. Slowly nailing our way upward, it took most of that day to ascend the next two hundred feet. The cracks were shallow, thin and just plain awkward, and drainage water trickled constantly from the overhangs above. In some places, the crack systems we were following disappeared and we had to perform wild pendulum swings across the face to find another way up. Often, the pegs went into the rock grudgingly and we had to trust our weight to RURPs, realized ultimate reality pitons, revolutionary tiny anchors with a blade length of just one centimeter. In other places we used sky-hooks, small metal claws that we hung from tiny bumps on the otherwise smooth rock face.

By the end of the day, we were both soaked, our wet clothes plastered to our cold skins. The circulation to my legs had been cut off by long hours cramped in my climbing harness. But after struggling up the rope, I pulled myself onto the first ledge of the day, to find Rusty already fast asleep. The ledge was a spacious two feet wide by four feet long, and we dubbed it the Palace. It turned out to be the biggest ledge on the whole climb! From that point onward, we spent most nights in hammocks anchored to the vertical rock.

Despite our choice of name, however, the ledge was desperately uncomfortable. The best I could do was to jam myself down the back of the knife edge, but the icy wet rock allowed little more than a prolonged doze. During the night, rainwater dripped in constant percussion off the overhangs above and trickled through the gaps in our bivouac bags. This scene was all too familiar to us. I found myself thinking increasingly of retreat.

The next day, as dawn broke and with the weather showing obvious signs of deterioration, we began the arduous descent down the ropes to the comforts of the valley below.

A week later, refreshed by rest and invigorated by clear skies, we returned once more to our high point and contemplated the blank rock above. Heading off from the Palace, I moved left on tiny ledges before placing a metal peg into a pocket in the rock. Hammering it into place only fractured the rock around it and, as I moved upward, the peg pulled out and tinkled down the rope toward Rusty, who was watching with a look of impending doom on his face. A fall here would have resulted in a wild swing. I was fifty feet above Rusty, and faced a fall of a hundred feet before he would stop my plunge on the rope.

Placing a skyhook on a small wrinkle of rock, I attached a foot loop and stepped up, my eyes riveted to the precarious anchor. Stretching up, I reached for a fingerhold and a tiny crack. Tapping in a centimeter-long RURP, I clipped in my rope before stretching across to a solid foothold. Hammering three metal pegs into deep cracks, I could finally breathe a sigh of relief.

Above, the way was blocked by a huge roof, an inverted staircase of overhangs stretching out horizontally for twenty-five feet. But now the rock was firmer, the cracks pronounced and deep. Climbing into a long, deep corner below the overhangs, I anchored myself and called for Rusty to follow.

Using special clamps to climb the rope, he slowly moved up to join me. Transferring all the hardware to his climbing harness, he started hammering pegs upward into the roof, swinging away from the rock, his feet in foot loops. Thirty minutes later, to our immense relief, he had overcome the obstacle and we were able to contemplate the route ahead.

Our radio contact that night brought us once more into the bosom of our friends in the valley. Climbing in mist throughout the day, we had felt very lonely and isolated. It was marvelous to be able to talk to Rusty's wife, Pat, and to hear his baby daughter gurgling into the speaker. To know that someone down below was caring for us came as a great tonic and relieved the monotony of our stark, overwhelming rock world.

For three days, we followed a line of perfect cracks toward the summit. In total control of ourselves and our world, we reveled in the increasing exposure, enjoying some of the

Rusty Baillie asleep on the Palace early in the climb of Sondre Trolltind.

best climbing of our careers. At night, we relaxed in the security of our hammocks under the stars as we awaited the pale golden glow of the dawn skies that would herald the coming day. The hardships were past, the rock dry and firm. We were becoming accustomed to living in this vertical world, and precaution was becoming a reflex. But now we had to become wary of overconfidence and complacency.

On the penultimate morning, as I was preparing to leave the bivouac, I unclipped my helmet from the rope where it had hung securely all night. The next second, before I knew what had happened, it was bouncing down the face, touching the rock once below my feet and then sweeping down in one huge arc before landing on the slabs at the foot of the wall two thousand feet below. Lost in mist, I could only trace its echo as it bounced down the thousands of feet of slabs to the valley floor. That day, I had plenty of time to reflect on the consequences of this mistake, which could perhaps prove to be serious.

With the good weather holding, the final morning dawned clear and we woke early. Eating all our spare food and leaving a cache of nonperishables for some future party, we climbed up the ropes, hauling the now much lighter sacks behind us. Although the rock was loose, the climbing was easy and we set off in high spirits for a rendezvous on the summit with a bottle of cognac.

And then followed near disaster! While removing an anchor, my hammering loosened a huge flake of rock, which detached itself from the face above. The next second, without realizing what had happened, I found myself dazed as a five-foot-square block struck my unprotected head, glanced off my shoulder and plummeted down the face with ever-increasing reverberations. Above, Rusty had instinctively braced himself, but the expected fall had never come. I was dangling on the rope, still held by my other anchor.

Faintly, I could hear Rusty calling me from above. "Are you okay, John?"

Looking down on Rusty Baillie from high on Sondre Trolltind.

"I don't know," I mumbled. "Give me a minute."

My head was swirling and I could feel the sticky warmth of blood trickling down my forehead. I had a searing pain in my left shoulder and felt sick to my stomach.

But we were more than four thousand feet up the cliff. There was no option but to keep climbing.

My mental resources had been shattered. The simplest climbing became hard, the firmest rock seemed loose. It was the closest I had ever come to a major climbing injury. From now on, I could not lead and the weight of responsibility fell to Rusty, but I could not have wished for a better companion in that situation. I put all my faith in him as he led me toward the summit, where we fell into the arms of our waiting Norwegian friends.

It was by far the hardest climb Rusty and I had ever done, but in the process, we forged a bond that one day would take us to Mount Everest together.

Without our innovative techniques, the climb would not have been possible. Our success changed the way Europeans pursued big wall climbing. The attempts together took seven days; five thousand feet of extreme climbing

Rusty Baillie and John Amatt on top of Sondre Trolltind.

consumed a total of fifty-five hours. Although many have since tried to climb the face on Sondre Trolltind, our route has only been repeated once. And the two young hot shots who made the climb described their ascent as desperately difficult!

In 1968, the year after climbing Sondre Trolltind, I graduated from teachers' college in Durham, a historic city in the north of England. It was during the three years I spent there that I started to understand the importance of precision teamwork in attaining goals in life. Having joined the rowing club upon my arrival, I was soon recruited to stroke the college eight, setting the rhythm for the rest of the crew to follow. One of the toughest of endurance sports, rowing demands a strict regimen of strength and fitness training, but success depends upon all eight crew members pulling the long oars through the water in perfect synchronization. Often, the winning team would not be the strongest or the fittest, but the one with the most coordinated technique.

Traditionally, the college rowing club had participated in weekend competitions throughout the region and had never competed farther afield. But in my final year, when I was elected Captain of Boats, I launched a funding drive, mailing thousands of letters to college alumni to solicit money to build a state-of-the-art racing shell, which would enable us to enter in the Henley Royal Regatta in southern England, perhaps the most prestigious international rowing event in the sport. Although we were beaten early in the competition by a more skillful university crew, Henley was an unforgettable experience, which proved, once again, that the effort counts more than the result. The willingness to innovate and to break new ground is always more significant than the outcome.

In a reference letter written by my mentor and college vice-principal, Dr. G.N.G. Smith, who we knew affectionately as "Ganges," he stated: "Mr. Amatt is a student of very good quality. Of strong and determined character and excellent background and appearance, he has academic ability above the average and a very strong sense of vocation. He takes his work seriously and organizes both himself and his studies efficiently and intelligently. He is a very hard worker. He is mature, co-operative and easy to get on with, so that he is generally popular both with staff and students. He is also very much of an individual, who thinks things out for himself, knows where he is going and is prepared to use his initiative and drive to get there. Perhaps at the moment slightly lacking in imagination, he is yet modest and unassuming; and, since he is a young man who learns readily from experience, his powers of imagination are likely to grow with increasing maturity. In character he is honest, truthful and entirely reliable; and he has a very pleasant sense of humour."

I have always treasured these words, particularly the reference to my being "slightly lacking in imagination." Today, I feel that my imagination is perhaps my greatest strength, an ability that I have developed through learning the lessons of experience, just as Ganges had predicted I would.

Having graduated with distinction as a teacher of physical education, I had to decide what I was going to do with the rest of my life. A couple of years previously, while I was in Peru, my sister had married and emigrated to Canada. I decided to join her in the province of Alberta, which was as close as I could get to the famous Canadian Rocky Mountains.

To achieve complete fulfillment in our lives, we must consciously be seeking out new experiences, not being content with the comfortable existence we have created through our previous efforts, but constantly seeking out new challenges and moving forward into the unknown.

FOUR

LEAVING THE BEATEN TRACK

Don't keep forever on the public road, going only where others have gone. Leave the beaten track occasionally and dive into the woods. You will be certain to find something you have never seen before. Of course it will be a little thing, but do not ignore it. Follow it up, explore all around it; one discovery will lead to another, and before you know it, you will have something worth thinking about to occupy your mind. All really big discoveries are the result of thought.
—*Alexander Graham Bell*

WHEN I LEFT ENGLAND, I was at the peak of my climbing career. Had I stayed, I would undoubtedly have become a professional mountaineer and taken part in many prestigious international expeditions, climbing with the best in Europe. But for some reason, I decided to give it all up. Perhaps it was my desire to keep moving into unknown territory, to create a sense of adventure, or the need to challenge myself in some new way. Perhaps it was my ambition to climb in North America. Whatever my reasons, the move to Canada filled me with excitement and I have never looked back.

When I arrived in the small prairie town of Medicine Hat, where I was to begin teaching, I was not disappointed. The down-to-earth farm people welcomed me with arms as open as the endless prairie skies. I enjoyed the social atmosphere, which was so much more casual than the rigid formality with which I had struggled in Britain.

Yet even on the prairies, the mountains seemed to control my destiny. Within a few days of my arrival, I saw a promotion for *The Magnificent Mountain*, the film we had made on Alpamayo a couple of years before. It had won an international award at the prestigious Trento Festival for Mountaineering and Exploration Films in Italy. It was being aired on Canadian national television the following week. Impulsively, I called the local station and they invited me to be interviewed.

It was there I met Peggy. She had grown up on a farm in nearby Saskatchewan and was employed at the television station writing advertising copy. Within a month we were engaged and, a year later when my parents arrived from England for a Christmas visit, we were married. For our honeymoon, we drove through the night to spend a couple of days near Banff, a world-renowned mountain resort in the Rockies.

At the time, I had become involved in organizing an international expedition to climb Mount Everest, which was set for 1971. However, because I had relocated in Canada, it became more and more difficult for me to coordinate such an immense project when most of its members lived in Europe. I was also beginning to have severe reservations about the cohesion of the team, which was made up of prima donna climbers from several countries, all of whom wanted to become the first from their nation to reach the top of the world. I was concerned about their individual willingness to make the personal sacrifices needed for success. So when Peggy and I were married, I resigned from the expedition.

Those first years in Canada were the most frustrating of my life. It was a struggle to establish myself in a new country where I knew so few people. Away from the mountains and cliffs of the British Isles, I was out of my element. During my summers away from teaching, I organized an outdoor adventure company, helped to start a weekly newspaper and attempted to establish an Outward Bound school. None of these ventures succeeded. At one very low point, I told Peggy that I felt I had done nothing with my life.

But in 1973, the year I became a Canadian citizen, I was offered a teaching job in the mountain town of Banff, right in the heart of the Canadian Rockies. I immediately jumped at the chance! In the mountains I was at home, and things started to take off.

At the high school in Banff, I introduced a new approach to learning by organizing arduous outdoor expeditions for the students, designed to build character by challenging physical adversity. In winter, we undertook multi-day ski tours in the subzero temperatures, sleeping in caves that we carved out of the snow. In summer, we would scale the highest peaks in the area, bivouacking on the summits to awaken to the glow of sunrise. The kids loved every minute.

To finance a month-long expedition to Baffin Island in the Canadian Arctic, we raised $10,000 by selling "Banff–Baffin" buttons at fifty cents apiece. The whole school became involved, even though only twelve students would be able to make the journey north. On that trip, we were able to make many ascents of previously unclimbed mountains and to explore a region of the Arctic never before visited by mountaineers.

This was to be the first of many visits to Baffin Island, during which I worked with Herb Bleuer, a mountain guide from Wengen in Switzerland, to train the local Inuit in mountain rescue techniques. In 1972, a section on the Cumberland Peninsula near the town of Pangnirtung had been designated as the world's first arctic national park. It is a superb wilderness of jagged peaks, rugged coastlines and ice-packed fjords, and attracts leading mountaineers from all over the world.

Hired as park wardens, the local Inuit had to be prepared to assist any visitors in difficulty. So for several years in the mid-1970s, Herb and I enjoyed flying northwards in the

Inuit children of Pangnirtung, Baffin Island, in Canada's Arctic.

late spring to work with these fun-loving people, often traveling by snowmobile across the ice floes to reach the mountains where the training was undertaken.

I had entered a new phase of my life.

Up until that point, I had been totally consumed with discovering who I was as a person. All of a sudden, I was helping others discover who they were and what they could do with their lives. People used to ask me what subjects I taught. I would reply, "I don't teach subjects, I teach kids." What was important to me was to help those children find what they were good at, to help them explore their potential the way I had explored mine through the mountains. But when the outdoor challenge program in Banff ran out of funding after just one year, I took another leap of faith into the unknown and quit teaching for good.

During the organization of the Baffin Island Expedition, I had become acquainted with Dr. David Leighton, who at that time was the director of The Banff Centre for Continuing Education. Renowned for its schools of fine arts and management, the Banff Centre had long planned a school of the environment, which would focus on developing innovative strategies for environmental decision-making in both public and private sectors. Hearing of my availability, Dr. Leighton approached me to take on the challenge of establishing the new school. I threw myself into the task, securing a $250,000 grant from a charitable foundation and rounding up faculty from throughout North America.

Since the school was located in Banff National Park, one of the world's most beautiful and ecologically important natural regions, it was obvious to me that we should offer programs that utilized the mountain environment in every way possible. During my unsuccessful attempt to start an Outward Bound school a few years earlier, I had pondered the possibility of using experiential, physical challenges as a way of bringing focus to management training. Here was the perfect opportunity to put my theories into practice. I soon recruited Joe Nold, who had been almost single-handedly responsible for the development of the Outward Bound movement in the United States, and together we wrote the original proposal for what were to become widely known as the Banff Wilderness Seminars.

The seminars were promoted as stress-management courses for top-level business executives. The focus of the seminars was essentially the same as for my high school programs: to help others discover their potential through mountain challenges. For several years, burned-out executives from all over North America met at secluded Skoki Lodge, a historic log cabin near Lake Louise, to enter into a ten-day process of self-discovery. I ran the outer journey, a physically demanding program of rock climbing, mountaineering and outdoor activities. My colleague, psychologist Dr. Layne Longfellow, ran the inner journey, a series of intense group discussions. Our objective was to develop the whole person; the experience had a dramatic effect.

Toward the end of the seminar, participants were required to spend twenty-four hours alone beneath a lean-to shelter they had constructed themselves. The assignment during this rare experience of isolation was to use the time to reflect on their learning of the previous days. It was during one such solo that a participant wrote:

> As I was shaping my walking stick to fit my hand, I started thinking that it resembled my life. I could start over at the top or, better still, I could start at any place I chose. Just as the wood was shaped many years ago in its rough, original form, so was my life shaped many years ago. I am

Management seminar participants reach their peak in the Canadian Rockies.

able to . . . smooth the rough edges . . . and perhaps reshape them to fit my new phase of life, just as I am cutting and reshaping the stick to fit my hand. It appears to me that as long as you have a good base to work with, you should be able to reshape that base to fit whatever you want. But be careful not to overshape it. Leave some of the original character of the base, something solid you can recognize.

With my walking stick, there was some danger from the knife as the rough parts were smoothed. I had to be careful. I am sure that I will have to be just as careful in smoothing and reshaping my new life. It will take some time. I must not hurry.

Here was a group of very successful, wealthy entrepreneurs, but, because of their commitment to work, their personal lives were often in ruins. They envied me for my lifestyle. It shocked me. I began to realize that we sometimes lack balance between the conflicting demands of modern society. The pressure to achieve professionally often overcomes the importance of family and of having a life of your own.

While I was at the Banff Centre, I also founded the Banff Festival of Mountain Films as a way of celebrating the mountain environment and the impact mountains can have on people's lives. It was an immediate success and is now the most important celebration of mountain life in the world. For almost twenty years, films on the mountain environment, mountain people and mountain sports have poured in from all over the world to compete for the festival's coveted awards. Every year, during the first weekend in November, thousands of mountain lovers jam the center's three theaters to gorge themselves on the festival's unique diet of excitement, adrenaline, and risk. Guest speakers through the years have been some of the leading figures in world mountaineering, people like Chris Bonington, Maurice Herzog and Reinhold Messner, the first man to climb Everest without using bottled oxygen.

Despite all these successes, however, there was still something missing from my life. While I had been teaching, I had never been able to focus on anything for more than a couple of years. The first year I would be fired with enthusiasm, but during the second year I would often lose interest when I found myself teaching things I had already taught. I am easily bored. I need to try new things and to be on the cutting edge, because if I am not, I start to stagnate. I need to know more and more about John Amatt, what he can do, what is his potential. At the time, what I needed was a new challenge.

In the years since I arrived in Canada, I had been striving to organize a major mountaineering expedition to the Himalayas, the highest range of mountains in the world. But I kept meeting roadblocks along the way. After pulling out of the 1971 international expedition, I had an opportunity to be part of a Canadian expedition to Mount Everest in 1975. To be led by Hans Gmoser, who pioneered helicopter skiing in the Bugaboos of British Columbia, that expedition collapsed when the federal government pulled its promised financial support. In 1976, the year our daughter Jillian was born, I got permission from the Nepalese government for an expedition to climb Mount Pumori, a 23,442-foot mountain in the Everest region. But even though the climb went ahead and was a success, I was unable to participate because of my obligations at the Banff Centre, and to my new family.

It was frustrating to be a visionary who was not able to carry out his dreams.

Finally, in 1979, I began talking with Bill March and Rusty Baillie, whom I had hired to work with me on the Banff Wilderness Seminars. I had known Bill from my early climbing days in Britain, and Rusty was my veteran friend from Sondre Trolltind. Now both were working in the physical education faculty at the University of Calgary. They had been invited to join a Canadian expedition to Mount Everest that was being planned for fall 1982.

When I was a young climber, it had been my ambition to climb Mount Everest. I had wanted to make my living as a professional mountaineer, and I knew if I could reach the summit of Everest, it would give me credibility in that field. Some seventeen years after I climbed the Troll Wall and initiated the journey, I would get to the mountain of my dreams.

We can't just drift through life and let the current carry us. There are demanding situations where you have to start paddling a little bit harder to alter your course, your speed, your direction. Ultimately, we are in control.

—*Sharon Wood*

FIVE

THE ULTIMATE CHALLENGE

*If you cannot understand that there is something in us that responds
to the challenge of this mountain and goes out to meet it, that the
struggle is the struggle of life itself—upward and forever upward—
then you won't see why we go. What we get from this adventure is
just sheer joy. And joy is, after all, the end of life. We do not live to
eat and make money. We eat and make money to be able to enjoy life.
That is what life means and what life is for.*

—George Leigh Mallory

MOUNT EVEREST IS THE
gold medal in the Olympic Games of mountaineering. At
29,028 feet, it is the tallest mountain in the world and represents the highest point of achievement for humans on the face
of the earth. Because of this, there will always be men and
women who want to climb it for themselves, no matter how
many times it has been climbed previously.

Sitting astride the border between Tibet to the north
and Nepal to the south, Everest is a huge mass of black, forbidding rock and ice that dominates the landscape in every
direction. Apart from its height, its appeal to mountaineers is
to be found in its unique heritage and history. When you
attempt to climb Mount Everest, you follow in the footsteps of
all the great mountaineers who have been there before you.

And there is probably more written about this mountain than any other. Everybody who has ever climbed has read a book about Everest.

The first expedition to attempt Everest was in 1924, when a somewhat oddly clad group of British mountaineers approached the mountain, wearing Harris tweed jackets, shirts and ties, and scarves wrapped around their necks. They wore thin leather boots with no insulation. To gain some traction on the slippery ice, they had to drive nails through the leather soles of their boots. They slept in tents with doors that had no effective closure system and they would often wake up in the morning with their sleeping bags covered in snow. And they carried oxygen cylinders made of solid steel, so that the negative effect of the weight quite possibly offset whatever positive benefit they were getting from breathing the oxygen. Despite their very rudimentary equipment, they almost reached the top of the world on that first attempt.

One of the leading climbers on this initial expedition was George Leigh Mallory, who became famous for his pert answer, "Because it's there!" when a reporter asked him why he wanted to climb Everest. But he also explained further by calling Everest "the struggle of life itself—upward and forever upward."

Tragically, Mallory disappeared on the expedition in 1924. He was last seen with his companion, Andrew Irvine, as they climbed into the clouds at 28,000 feet. They were never seen again, and for many years the debate has raged about whether they might have reached the summit twenty-nine years before Edmund Hillary and Tenzing Norgay made the first confirmed ascent in 1953.

Some fifty years after Mallory and Irvine disappeared, a Chinese climber, Wang Kow Po, attempted to climb the northern route on Everest pioneered by the British. He discovered a body frozen in the ice high on the side of the mountain at 26,500 feet. When he touched the clothes of the dead, they broke into pieces and were blown away by the wind. Unaware

The north face of Everest, where Mallory and Irvine disappeared in 1924.

of the controversy surrounding Mallory and Irvine, he buried the body in the snow and moved on. Five years later, Wang Kow Po died in an avalanche on a return visit to Everest, before he was able to pinpoint where he had seen the body.

The speculation today is that the body must be Mallory or Irvine. But the question is whether the climber died on the way down from a successful summit ascent or had succumbed to the rarefied air while struggling toward the top of the world. Several expeditions have since searched for the body, but Everest is so huge that the chances of finding it again are slim. It is known that the two climbers were carrying a camera, and the theory is that the film must have been frozen all these years. If the camera can be found and the film processed, we may be able to discover where the last photograph was taken.

I have often asked myself how men with such rudimentary equipment and lack of high-altitude experience could do so well on that first attempt on Everest. I think the answer is that they just didn't know any better! No mountaineers had been there before. Nobody had discovered the physical risks of high altitude. They had no mental barriers to impose upon themselves. So they went to the mountain with completely open minds. They moved forward with a positive attitude and optimism—and they almost reached the summit.

In September 1979, I was invited to join the Canadian expedition to Mount Everest as a climber and as business manager. I was thirty-four, and my personal aspirations had changed. Although I had often dreamed of standing on the summit of Everest, I knew that my role on this climb would be different. I became involved simply to make sure the expedition was properly financed and organized. I wanted to do everything I could to give the team the optimum chance of success because when one person reaches the top, everyone on the team climbs the mountain. For the next two years, I traveled back and forth across Canada, knocking on the doors of hundreds of companies to seek sponsorship of our climb. My salary was a scant $250 a week.

Organizing and funding an expedition to Mount Everest is rather like establishing and running a small corporation. One of our first tasks was to raise money. When I came on board, the only revenue the expedition had secured was $25,000, earned from the sale of the exclusive newspaper and magazine rights to the upcoming story. Having been involved in the early stages of the 1971 expedition, I realized that it would be critical to our success to find a major corporate sponsor who would be willing to pick up a large percentage of the overall cost and to lend credibility and public exposure to the expedition. We began our search by calling a press conference in Calgary.

By coincidence, Mike Breckon was flying across the country that very day. He was the newly appointed advertising director of Air Canada. As he flew, he was writing notes to himself about possible promotional projects for the airline. British-born, he had been in London in 1953 at the Coronation of Queen Elizabeth II and still remembered the excitement when news filtered down through the crowd that the British had climbed Everest for the first time. Impulsively, he wrote down "Everest" on his list, thinking that it would be a suitable long-term promotion for the airline, not knowing of our plans. That night, he checked into his Toronto hotel room and picked up a copy of the local newspaper. A headline caught him by surprise. "Canadians to Climb Everest: Looking for Corporate Sponsor." Immediately, he picked up the phone and called our office at the University of Calgary.

As can be imagined, Air Canada had to be very cautious about sponsoring such a potentially risk-filled endeavor and aligning itself with a relatively unknown group of people. It took a year and a half of negotiations and numerous trips to the airline's head office in Montreal before we finally signed a contract for exclusive corporate sponsorship of the expedition. They would provide $280,000 in cash over three years, plus free air service for all climbers and a cargo plane to fly all of our supplies to Nepal.

In today's economy, when funds are raised for any kind of project, it is essential to offer something tangible in return. To benefit from the investment, Air Canada needed wide public exposure to promote its sponsorship. At the time, the airline was initiating a new air route to the Indian subcontinent, and reasoned that a high-profile Everest expedition would draw public attention to that part of the world. Just as important, Air Canada had a corporate philosophy that was based upon six key values and beliefs: professionalism, teamwork, integrity, candor, equality and adaptability. Air Canada's management recognized that these were the qualities that would be needed if our expedition was to get to the top of Mount Everest.

Mike Breckon was in the right seat of the right corporation at the right time. If it were not for his enduring support and Air Canada's sponsorship, it is very likely that this

Air Canada advertisement announcing its sponsorship of the 1982 Canadian Mount Everest Expedition.

expedition, which was to have such a profound impact on my life, would never have taken place.

With Air Canada's support, we were able to move into a new phase of our preparations. Together with George Kinnear, at that time the team's climbing leader (he was subsequently forced to resign due to retinal damage to his eyes caused by high-altitude climbing), I flew to England to consult with Chris Bonington, who had led two large expeditions to Everest's difficult southwest face in 1972 and 1975. In addition, we met with Sir Edmund Hillary and flew out to Kathmandu to lay the foundation for our climb with Bobby Chettri, the highly efficient outfitter whose company, Nepal Himal, now organizes commercial treks throughout the valleys and villages of the Himalaya Mountains.

Seeking an aerial reconnaissance of Everest while in Kathmandu, we chartered a small, supercharged Pilatus Porter aircraft and flew with world-famous pilot Emil Wick over Everest's summit at thirty thousand feet. Since the plane was not pressurized, we had to wear oxygen masks throughout the flight, and we flew in the subzero temperatures with an open door to facilitate clear photography of the mountain and the route that we planned to climb. As the plane climbed higher into the jet-stream winds, it was tossed about with increasing regularity, so much so that at one point I found myself more out of the plane than in, as a major gust knocked the plane onto its side. One look down onto the desolate world of ice and snow below and I hauled myself back inside the plane, thankful that my lap belt had held me in place.

To enhance our credibility, I also approached the Right Honorable Roland Michener, former Governor-General of Canada and Canadian Ambassador to India and Nepal, to become our patron. At our first meeting in an oak-paneled private club in Toronto, he told me that Mount Michener, a 9,843-foot peak in the Canadian Rockies, was named after him. I recalled that some years before, Robert Kennedy had climbed Mt. Kennedy in Alaska, a mountain that had been

Right Honourable Roland Michener on the summit of Mount Michener in the Canadian Rockies.

named for his brother, John F. Kennedy. So I asked, "Why don't you consider climbing Mount Michener with us as part of our training program?" He jumped at the chance, even though he was more than eighty years old at the time. During spring 1981, Mr. Michener became our patron and a few months later reached the top of Mount Michener at the age of eighty-two. Amazingly, we found no signs on the summit that the mountain had been previously climbed. He had made the first ascent!

In a subsequent special edition of *Travel Times* magazine, published to commemorate the Everest climb, Roland Michener commented: "Why should [they] now be undertaking this ultimate challenge to their skill and daring? Certainly not because the experience of many expeditions and the aid of modern science has made it safe to climb Mount Everest. The answer can be found in the indomitable will to discover and excel [that is a part of our nature as human beings]. . . .

"As an advocate of . . . sport and physical fitness for all who would enjoy a full and healthy life, I believe that great achievements by such as the Canadian Everest climbers, set the essential example and inspiration to the multitudes who [would follow in their footsteps and] seek excellence."

Although our Everest team included some of the most accomplished technical climbers in Canada, at the time we had limited experience of climbing at extreme elevations. The highest mountain in Canada, Mount Logan in the Yukon, is only 19,850 feet high. When the permit to climb Mount Everest was first granted by the Nepalese authorities in 1978, the highest mountain Canadians had ever climbed was Mount Pumori in the Everest region, 23,442 feet high. As part of our preparation, I proposed a training program of mini expeditions designed to put every member of the team above 20,000 feet in the year prior to the Everest expedition, even though this would add considerably to my funding challenge. As a result of this initiative, we executed eight different training expeditions to peaks in Alaska, Argentina, Nepal and western China, all of which took place in 1981.

During this training, I seized the opportunity to lead a four-man team to attempt a ski ascent of Mount Muztagata, a 24,757-foot-high mountain in Xinjiang province of western China. On the map, this area is identified as being "in dispute," and fighting still occurs in border tangles between China, Afghanistan and Pakistan. The previous year, an American party had skied all the way to the summit of Muztagata; Lloyd Gallagher, Pat Morrow, Stephen Bezruchka and I wanted to repeat this ascent, but by a different route.

We flew into Beijing in August 1981 and amused ourselves by carrying skis during a visit to the Great Wall of China. One can imagine the quizzical looks we received from the hordes of Chinese and Western tourists as we donned our equipment and attempted to make the first ski descent of this famous landmark. Descending the steep stone staircases that form much of this imposing structure, I passed a group of Americans who were heard to comment: "Where the hell did they come from?" when they observed us clad in ski boots and carrying downhill skis over our shoulders.

Continuing across the vast and featureless Gobi and Takla Makan deserts, we arrived at Kashgar, a city of 175,000, composed mainly of Uigir people, one of the fifty-five minority nationalities of China. Our visit took us back to a time when Kashgar was a center for the Silk Road that linked Cathay with Persia in the East and Rome in the West. Transportation today is still by rickety donkey cart; the carts compete with the occasional dilapidated tractor and drab government-green Jeep.

Loading our eight hundred pounds of equipment and food aboard a run-down, dust-filled bus, we embarked on the 120-mile, bone-jarring drive that took us to base camp at the

Lloyd Gallagher "skiing" the Great Wall of China.

foot of Muztagata. Several days later, a team of camels arrived, snorting in bad-tempered disgust and spitting regurgitated grass at their Kirghiz masters. Clinging atop our skis and supplies, we swayed and jerked our way to the foot of the mountain, where we could start to ski upward. That night, sleeping alone in a tent at seventeen thousand feet as a snowstorm howled outside, I suffered from nightmares, dreaming that I was suffocating in the thin air. Awakening with a start, I was forced to sit up to regain my breath—a problem that did not bode well for the climb to come.

Ten days later, we were within striking distance of the summit.

Each morning, we had lain dozing in the warmth of our sleeping bags, awaiting the sun that would bring life to our freezing world. As the rays reached the tent, the hoarfrost lining the fabric—our frozen breath of the previous night—began to melt, dripping onto the chaos of sleeping bags, foam mattresses, packs, cameras, cook pots and stoves, where the four of us had squeezed during the previous night, twisting relentlessly in search of comfort.

One by one we slipped out of our bags. Donning only boots and jackets, since we had slept fully clothed for the warmth, we crawled through the tent door and fumbled with frozen skis. Thirty minutes later, our packs loaded with supplies, our skis clamped to special plastic and foam climbing boots, we started to ski slowly uphill. Synthetic sealskin fastened to the base of the skis gave us purchase on the soft snow as we climbed in long zigzags.

On the penultimate day, we rested in our tents, melting snow continuously and forcing ourselves to drink tea, hot juice and soup laced with canned meat and dehydrated vegetables. At these elevations, the air is so dry that dehydration is extreme.

In the early afternoon, as I tried to drink some hot chocolate, I was violently sick, losing all the precious liquids that I had been so carefully conserving in my stomach.

Skiing up Muztagata.

Immediately, my pulse dropped and I turned as white as a ghost, despite the sunburn of the previous days. Stephen, our doctor, ordered me to lie flat with my feet elevated. My color returned. But I remained dangerously weak from the experience.

The next morning dawned clear and we rose in the −30°F temperature to begin the summit attempt. I felt colder than ever as I followed Pat, who was breaking the trail that day. All the previous night, I had worried that I would not be strong enough to complete the climb. I soon had my answer. I felt pathetically weak and could feel the onset of frostbite in my fingers. To have continued might have jeopardized the climb for Steve, Lloyd or Pat, since one of them would have had to accompany me back if I had to retreat from higher up.

Turning back, I was disappointed but had few regrets. Such things happen at high altitude, when the body is on the knife edge. One of the important things about climbing mountains is the opportunity it affords for coming to grips with one's limitations. The struggle teaches us to accept reality.

As I skied slowly to the tent, the others continued upward, reaching the windswept summit after great effort, pushing their weary bodies to the limit of endurance until the goal was reached. But it had been a close call. On returning to the tent, Lloyd collapsed, utterly exhausted. It was more than an hour before he could summon the strength to drink the tea that I had prepared. The long-elusive summit had obviously drawn a great deal from each of us.

In a subsequent article published in Air Canada's *enRoute* magazine, I wrote: "Next year it will be Everest. Who knows what trials lie in wait for us there? One thing is certain, however: on Everest, it will be harder. A lot harder. For the difficulties on the world's highest mountain will scarcely have begun by the time we reach an altitude equivalent to the summit of Muztagata. And it will be a different kind of challenge, involving more people, a longer climb, at greater altitudes, but with a more sophisticated range of support systems: Sherpa guides, oxygen, extensive back-up supplies and personnel at base camp. The mountain may win. But whatever happens, the Everest attempt will be the challenge of our lives. This climb to the 29,028-foot summit of the world will take us closer to the limits of endurance than ever before; closer than any of us have ever dreamed possible."

In retrospect, my comments could not have been more prophetic.

Once you have started something, you must keep striving, learning, and adapting, no matter what setbacks you might experience along the way.

During the struggle to organize the Everest climb, I faced rejection every day, but I kept going because my intuition told me I was on the right path. Just knowing what you are doing

Mount Everest.

In the Western Cwm.

is right and then committing all your resources to the task is what makes things happen. There will always be people who are pessimistic and will try to put you down. But if you believe in what you are doing, you can use their negative energy as a catalyst to push yourself on and prove them wrong.

Finally, after five years of effort, we had recruited more than a hundred companies and individual supporters and raised more than one million dollars in funding. More than twenty tons of equipment and food had been assembled in bulk and repackaged into color-coded boxes destined for the four camps we would have to establish on Everest.

Following a raucous farewell party with family and friends around the fire pit behind our home in Canmore, Alberta, we left Canada on July 17, 1982, and flew halfway around the earth to Kathmandu, Nepal. Seven days later we set out on the three-week walk that would take us to the base of Mount Everest.

The hike to Mount Everest follows a 150-mile trail, winding from Kathmandu at 4,000 feet to base camp at 17,600 feet. The trail is constantly rising and falling as it cuts across five mountain ranges, so that you actually climb a total of 44,000 feet and descend some 30,000 feet before you even get to the bottom of Everest, where the real climbing begins. The walk can be done in as little as two weeks, but we took three, traveling at a leisurely pace to ease our acclimatization to the increasingly thin air.

Because we wanted to begin climbing as soon as possible after the monsoon rains, which last from June until August, we began walking in at the tail end of the monsoon season. It rained constantly. What would begin as a light afternoon drizzle would become a drenching downpour by evening. It often rained more than two inches a day, and we found ourselves wading along trails that had become raging torrents.

The constant humidity provided ideal conditions for the local leeches, which were constantly falling on us from overhanging branches or crawling in under our clothing. They were so insidious that they could slip through the lace holes of our boots, through the knitting of our socks, into the restaurant between our toes. As we hiked, they would be sucking our blood, getting fatter and fatter. Often, they would burst under the constant pressure of our feet pounding along the trail. There was no doubt that we became quite attached to them as the hike progressed. Our only protection was saltshakers, which were regulation issue for each climber. A shower of salt and the leech would shrivel and drop to the ground.

After two weeks on the trail, we arrived at Namche Bazar, a village 11,300 feet above sea level that is the largest community for the hardy Sherpa people who live high in the foothills of the Himalayas. Originally from Tibet, the name *Sherpa* is derived from the Tibetan word *Shar-pa*, meaning "easterner." Around four hundred years ago, a small group crossed into Nepal and settled in the upper valleys south and

Dave Read (left), John Amatt and Bill March (right) resting in the village of Jorsale below Everest.

west of Everest. Scattered in small communities throughout the area, they now live at elevations of between 10,000 and 15,000 feet.

The Sherpas are perfectly adapted to living at these elevations and it gives them a tremendous adaptive advantage over western mountaineers. Because of the constant exposure, their bodies are much better equipped for breathing the rarefied air, giving them more strength to bring to the challenge of climbing to the top of the world.

From an early age, the Sherpas travel everywhere on foot and carry everything on their backs. There are no roads within a hundred miles of their villages. It is not unusual to see the Sherpanis, the Sherpa women, carrying one-hundred-pound loads up and down the sides of tortuous mountain trails, supporting the weight solely with a strap across the top of their heads. In fact, we often observed these women running up the mountain trails, carrying huge loads that we could not even lift.

In planning for our expedition, we had accepted a very significant limitation compared to these Sherpas. The highest mountain in North America is Denali (Mount McKinley) in Alaska, 20,332 feet above sea level. Everest is nearly two miles higher. So while we recognized our technical abilities as mountaineers, we knew that we did not have the strength of the Sherpas at high altitudes.

At 29,028 feet, Everest climbs through two-thirds of the earth's atmosphere. As you gain height, the air gets thinner and thinner. By the time you are pushing for the summit, your body is getting about a quarter of the oxygen it could expect at sea level. This means that every little thing you do takes longer—in fact, every thought, every conversation, every physical act can take four times as long at the top of the mountain.

Since the air is getting thinner, it is also becomes increasingly dry and your body starts to dehydrate. As you climb higher, you lose between four to six liters of fluid from your body into the dry air each day. Over the six weeks it took

Sherpani and child.

Ceremony with the monk at the monastery at Tengboche.

to climb Mount Everest, every one of us was to lose twenty to thirty pounds.

It really is a great place to lose weight, but you are also losing strength. First, you lose your body fats, then your muscle tissue. As a result, you get weaker and weaker as you move higher and higher into this unpredictable, uncertain world.

Because we had acknowledged that we could not perform as effectively on Everest as the local people, we also knew that if we were to have any chance of success, we would have to integrate the Sherpas into our team. In effect, we needed their strengths to offset our limitations. Sherpas are commonly hired as porters and guides for Himalayan expeditions. But because of the events that were to transpire on our climb, our relationship with them was to develop into much more than a traditional employer-employee exchange.

The Sherpa people are Buddhist. They have their own name for Everest. They call it Chomolungma, "Mother Goddess of the Earth." For them, the mountain is sacred.

Perched on a grassy ridge above Namche Bazar is the monastery at Tengboche. Before starting out for base camp, it is traditional for the Sherpas to take part in a ceremony at the monastery, during which the monk blesses them and gives them good luck charms. They can then begin their approach to Everest with the knowledge that they have taken care of their spiritual needs.

This ceremony had little significance to us, because we did not understand the Buddhist faith, the Sherpa language or the symbolism of the event. But we went out of our way to share the ceremony in order to show our respect for the Sherpa people, their values and beliefs. It was a vital part of forging the bonds of trust between the two groups that would make up our team, one from the East and one from the West, as we struggled together to climb to the top of the world.

But we also knew the monastery at Tengboche from a previous visit. Some five years before the expedition took place, when we had first come to Nepal to reconnoiter for the climb, we visited a monk at the monastery. After studying some religious texts, he had made a prediction that we would carry in the back of our minds throughout our preparation. He told us that the year of our climb would be a disastrous one.

"There will be bad spirits on Chomolungma in 1982," he had said. "Many men and women will die trying to climb the mountain during the year of your attempt."

We knew that Everest is a dangerous mountain. In addition to the medical hazards of oxygen deprivation, the summit is guarded by treacherous ice slopes, unpredictable avalanches and rockfalls and glaciers riddled with deep crevasses. In winter, the jet stream can drop below 26,000 feet, and winds at the summit reach 130 or 140 miles an hour. Often, the temperature is as low as −50°F.

Although today more than five hundred individuals have reached the summit, more than one hundred and fifteen climbers and Sherpas have died in the attempt, with one-third of all fatalities being the native people. That means that for every four or five who go all the way, one person is destined to die trying. Of course, there are thousands of others who take part in Everest expeditions and never reach the summit. Nonetheless, the chances of tragedy are very real.

We accepted the danger and knew of the prediction. But we could not allow the fear of what might be to stop us from moving toward our goal. For most of us, this might be our only chance to attempt Everest, and we had to put our faith in our ability to minimize the dangers by using our experience and resourcefulness to make the climb as safe as possible.

We were confident that we could adapt to any situation we might face.

Your moment of strength is when you have the greatest amount of singleness of purpose.

—*Laurie Skreslet*

SIX

LEARNING FROM SETBACKS

You gain strength, courage, and confidence by every experience in which you really stop to look fear in the face . . . the danger lies in refusing to face the fear, in not daring to come to grips with it . . . You must make yourself succeed every time. You must do the thing you think you cannot do.

—Eleanor Roosevelt

ON AUGUST 15, 1982, AFTER three weeks of walking, we finally arrived at the base of Everest at 17,600 feet, where the real climbing would begin.

Base camp is a thoroughly unpleasant place! It has become the dump of forty years of expeditions to the mountain. In some ways, however, it is also a living museum of mountaineering. We found ladders used by the Japanese and titanium oxygen tanks probably used by the Russians, who had climbed a new route on the mountain the previous spring. The oxygen cylinder with the Union Jack on it may have been from the British Southwest Face team of 1975, or possibly even from the British Everest Expedition of 1953, which had put Hillary and Tenzing on the summit for the first time.

But there is also garbage and human waste left behind by previous groups, which has polluted the water supply.

It took a few days to get our water purification system to function and, in our rush to come to grips with the climb, we made the mistake of drinking the icy water without adequately cleansing it. Immediately we all came down with enteric dysentery, from which I never fully recovered. I was constantly exhausted; it usually took me three or four hours longer to carry a load of equipment to the upper camps than other members of the team.

The morning after our arrival, the Sherpas erected a tall pole in the center of camp and started to build a small altar at its base. Here they would burn juniper brought up from the valley below in order to safeguard the expedition through the coming days.

Draping the structure in prayer flags, the Sherpas began a ritualistic ceremony involving the consumption of large

Everest base camp.

amounts of food and drink. It was essential that our climbing team took part in this ceremony so we could show our respect for the religious beliefs of the local people. We were soon caught up in the party fervor. At 17,600 feet, a little bit of alcohol can go a long way. We already had headaches from the lack of oxygen at these altitudes. Now we were really to suffer. It took several days to recover from the high-altitude hang-overs, but having made our sacrifice to the mountain gods, we were ready to start the climb.

Because of our limited experience at high altitude, in choosing our strategy we had opted for a classic siege of the mountain. This involved establishing four camps, the last at 26,200 feet. It would be from this camp that a summit bid would be launched.

Our approach was simple. First, the strongest climbers would push the route forward until they located a safe camp-site. Then this route would be fixed with rope anchored to aluminum stakes driven into the ice and snow. Over the course of the expedition, our team would fix more than five miles of rope to safeguard our descent. Last, the climbers and Sherpas would carry loads of food and equipment on their backs along the fixed route to equip the upper camps. Altogether, it would take more than a month before all the supplies were carried into place.

The logistical plan took the form of a pyramid, with a broad base of support at base camp, tapering to less and less support as the final camp was established 2,800 feet below the summit. Base camp would have twelve tons of equipment and fifteen climbers, five support personnel and twenty-nine Sherpa porters, while the highest camp, Camp IV might require only ten forty-pound loads for a summit bid by two to four climbers.

To get to Camp I, we had to pass through a treacherous, tumbling glacier known as the Khumbu Icefall, which we knew to be the most dangerous part of the climb. It was here that we were to learn the true meaning of the word *commitment*.

Climbing in the Khumbu Icefall.

We cannot allow the fear of what might be to stop us from moving toward our goals in life.

The Khumbu Icefall is the most unpredictable place on Everest. It is a two-thousand-foot-high cascade of shifting pillars and tottering cathedrals of ice. As the glacier moves down a steep grade, it splits apart, opening deep crevasses. The ice is constantly moving at an average speed of two to three feet a day. Occasionally it can move a foot in two hours. At other times, it can lurch forward ten feet in one second, toppling blocks of ice the size of houses. We knew that more climbers died in this place than anywhere else on the mountain.

There are no guarantees of anything in the Icefall, but it is necessary to establish a workable route through this maze so the camps can be provisioned before the summit bid is launched.

The most dangerous place we encountered was a severely disrupted area we dubbed the Traverse, where we were forced to move horizontally across the fall line of the ice for some two hundred yards. Although it was the safest route we could find in that zone, it was not safe by any stretch of the imagination. In the words of one climber: "Basically, there was nothing there but thirty-foot ice towers above and one-hundred-fifty-foot-deep crevasses below. Our route lay about twenty feet below the general elevation of the Icefall, along chunks of ice that had fallen and become wedged in the crevasse. There was a lot more air than substance to what we were trying to move across, and what substance there was kept sinking further into the air."

In order to minimize the dangers, we bridged the crevasses with aluminum ladders and fixed ropes through all the unpredictable places. It was common knowledge where the most treacherous places were and we would rush through as fast as possible. With forty-pound packs on our backs, we would end up collapsing on the far side, taking up to fifteen minutes to recover from the effort. We even started getting up in the darkness of the early morning, theorizing that in the cold of the night the ice would be more solidly frozen and less liable to surge forward.

To this day, I can remember waking up to the shrill of my alarm sounding in the darkness at 2:00 a.m. Relishing the warmth of my sleeping bag, it often took a conscious effort to force myself to face the challenges that I knew the day would bring. Shivering in the −20°F temperatures, I would climb out of the tent and stagger across the broken rocks toward the kitchen tent, where I would drink numerous cups of tea and juice to offset the dehydration that was occurring constantly at this elevation. Then, not really wanting to go but knowing I must, I would force myself to leave behind this relative comfort and head out into a world of frozen darkness.

As I climbed through the ice in the dark, my narrow world lit only by the beam of my headlamp, I could feel the creaking and groaning of the ice under my feet. I could see cracks appearing in the snow that had not been there the day before. And I would note how the ropes were starting to stretch under the tension of the moving ice. In some places, the aluminum ladders were twisted and bent by the pressure of a crevasse closing from both sides. Even at night, this was not a safe place to be!

In retrospect, it is clear that if this had not been Everest, we would never have gone anywhere near that Icefall. But because it was Everest, we took chances that we would not have considered on lesser mountains.

Before the expedition left Canada, a friend had given me a St. Christopher medallion. The medallion had been with him all his life and he asked me to take it and bring it (and myself) back safely from Mount Everest. Coincidentally, my sister had also given me a St. Christopher. I was greatly touched by their gestures. All the time I was in the Icefall, I had one of these medallions hanging around my neck and the other in my pocket.

One day, as I was preparing to go back up through the broken ice, I found that I had lost one of the medals. I panicked in the realization that I had lost a friend's treasured possession and my own psychological crutch. My mind was in turmoil, my heart thumping wildly, and it took me nearly half an hour to calm down. Finally, I was able to rationalize that I had lost the medallion in the Icefall and it was still there to protect me as I went through. I am not a religious person, but I found myself praying in this area quite regularly.

There was only one time when I came close to having an accident in that precarious place. Descending the fixed lines one day, I heard a sharp crack behind me. Startled, I looked up and saw an ice cliff the size of a house breaking away about a hundred feet directly above me. Turning, I raced down the rope as fast as I could, but before I had gone very far, I hit an anchor in the line and was forced to stop. Frantically, I looked around. The whole cliff had collapsed and buried the rope where I had

John Amatt climbing in the Khumbu Icefall.

been standing seconds before. Luckily, it had not continued downhill after me.

When I think about those days in the Icefall, I realize the only real advantage we had in going through in the dark was that we were unable to see just how deep the crevasses were, because the ice was still moving downhill at night. It was a place of extreme unpredictability; it was the gateway to Everest, however, and we had no choice but to pass through if we were to achieve our goal.

After two weeks of effort, we occupied our first camp-site at 19,600 feet, above the dangers of the Khumbu Icefall. This was a great day for the expedition. Everything was going well. We had found a reasonably safe route through the moving ice and were very optimistic about an early success.

Looking back, I feel we were starting to build a bubble of invincibility around ourselves. Without realizing it, we were already becoming a little complacent, focusing on the summit without really paying attention to what was going on around us. We were entering into the most dangerous period of the climb!

That night, strong winds blew deep snow onto the upper slopes of Everest, high above our heads. The tents at Camp I were covered with a heavy blanket, which had to be cleared away every hour throughout the night. Strangely, however, no snow fell down at base camp, where most of our team were sleeping.

In the early hours of the morning, fifteen climbers and Sherpas set out in the darkness to climb through the Icefall toward Camp I. By the time they were well into the Icefall, they found themselves pushing through fresh snow. Even more troubling were the strong winds, which made the newly deposited snow very unstable.

Just before five o'clock in the misty dawn, a slab of snow slowly fell away from the west shoulder of Everest, far above. Hearing a noise like thunder, the party paused to listen. It was not unusual to hear an avalanche falling. We had heard many since we arrived at base camp, but they had all faded away into the distance. This one didn't. It thundered louder and louder as it came closer. But because of the mist, it was impossible to tell from which direction it was coming. The noise was echoing around and around the valley.

As the avalanche roared toward the climbers, it was forcing the air out of its path. The blast of wind hit the group, knocking them off their feet and blowing them twenty feet through the air until the ropes pulled tight. Then out of the mist came the bowling mass of snow and ice, which scythed right through the line of men, burying seven who were in its path.

That morning, I had been sleeping in at base camp, enjoying a rest day. I was awakened from a deep sleep by a sudden gust of wind that set my tent flapping. But I thought nothing of it; I just rolled over and continued to doze. Suddenly, Lloyd Gallagher, who had been manning the radio connection with the Icefall team, came running across from the kitchen tent and thrust his head through the door flap.

"There's been an avalanche," he shouted. "Get up! Now!"

While a rescue party scrambled up through the ice to help, Lloyd and I coordinated the effort from base camp. Over and over we called on the radio into the darkness, but received no reply. It was a horrible time. No one knew what had happened. At one point, nine team members were missing. Finally, one by one, the climbers checked in and, by process of elimination, we discovered three Sherpas had disappeared.

The avalanche had begun some five thousand feet above the Icefall. At its widest point, it measured more than a mile. As the snow fell off the west shoulder of Everest, it billowed up with enough force to sift powder snow down onto base camp, nearly two miles below. It was that blast of wind that had rattled my tent and woken me up.

The snow had settled like cement at the accident site. It took three hours to dig through the debris before uncovering the first body. It was Pasang Sona, a forty-year-old Sherpa who had been to Everest many times. Pasang Sona was a man who knew the dangers of this mountain better than most and who had accepted personal responsibility for his decision to go back one more time. He was also a husband, father and provider for his family. Now, after three hours lying crushed beneath ice and snow, Pasang Sona was dead. We tried everything we could to bring him back to life. Rusty Baillie climbed into a sleeping bag with him in a vain attempt to reheat his body; Steve Bezruchka, one of our expedition doctors, performed CPR and mouth-to-mouth resuscitation. But three hours was just too long. The bodies of twenty-year-old Ang Tsultim and forty-year-old Dawa Dorje were never found. To this day, they lie buried in the ice of Everest.

"It was shattering," says Baillie. "It's one thing to sit in a bar and say, 'Geez, you know twenty-four men have died in that Icefall; we'll have to be very careful in there.' It's quite another to be carrying the body of a friend down through it."

All of a sudden our bubble of invincibility had burst. The worst possible thing had happened. Three people were dead! I felt hollow and sick. I remember stepping outside the tent. It was a gray, misty dawn, silent except for the soft hiss of the falling snow. As I waited, the rescue party brought down the body of Pasang Sona on a stretcher.

I don't think we had really appreciated the seriousness of the climb until this moment. For about three years prior to our expedition, there had been no accidents recorded on Mount Everest. We had begun to think this climb was not as dangerous as we had been led to believe. It had seemed like a big holiday for most of us. We'd payed lip service to the possibility that somebody might get killed, but now we had to face the terrible reality.

Without adversity, without change, life is boring.
The paradox of comfort is that we stop trying.

I thought: Shit! The media will sit up and take notice. We've really got a tiger by the tail. This was going to be big news. I started to think about the implications for the sponsors, for the media and for the Canadian public. I was particularly

Carrying down the body of Pasang Sona.

The cremation of Blair Griffiths.

concerned that our friends and relatives back in Canada be assured that we were safe. We needed to get the facts out before people started speculating and distorting the whole thing. But the problem was that our radio link between base camp and Kathmandu was tenuous at best. The closest working radio was in the National Park Office at Namche Bazar, a two-day walk away.

A monk came up from the nearby monastery and prayed over Pasang Sona's body through the long dark hours. At dawn, Bill March, Steve Bezruchka and a team of Sherpas carried the body down to the village of Lobuche for cremation. I accompanied them and then continued down the valley on my own to radio out a detailed report on the accident to the Nepalese authorities in Kathmandu.

As I was going down a steep hill below the village, I heard a terrible sound coming up the trail toward me. It was the wife and family of one of the dead Sherpas. As she approached me, the woman sank to her knees and grasped my legs. She was wailing and crying. It was impossible to understand what she was saying. All I could say was, "I'm sorry. I'm just so sorry." I didn't have the words to say anything else because I knew that if we had not been attempting to climb Everest that day, those Sherpa men might still be alive.

Finally, the others in the group led her away. But the cries of that woman remain with me to this day.

Being Buddhist, the Sherpas believe in karma, which we in the West might call destiny, or fate. They also believe in reincarnation. They later told us, "The avalanche was just one of those things! It was meant to be!" They said if Pasang Sona hadn't died on Everest that day, he would have died somewhere else because it was his day to journey into the next life.

There were no recriminations, just a feeling of shared sorrow and concern for the expedition. The Sherpas accepted the inevitability of this tragedy. They never once suggested anybody was to blame. In fact, they encouraged us to continue with the climb.

That night, I slept in the home of a Sherpa family in the village of Pheriche and continued down to Namche Bazar the next morning. With considerable difficulty, I was able to establish radio contact with the government officials in Kathmandu. Just as I was terminating the call, I heard a faint message crackling down from Lobuche. It was Bill March. There had been another accident on the mountain!

While Bill and Steve had been attending the cremation of Pasang Sona's body, a group of climbers had returned to the Icefall to start repairing the sections of the route that had been buried by the avalanche. Four men had paused in the Traverse to straighten a twisted ladder that bridged a gaping crevasse. As they worked, the glacier suddenly shifted! A whole section of ice toppled forward twenty feet, crumbling under the forces unleashed from above. As huge blocks of ice toppled into a crevasse, Rusty Baillie leaped from block to block in a dance for his life.

Dave Read was not so lucky. He lost his balance and fell headfirst down a long roller coaster into the deep blue hole. As the ice settled, he found himself upright with his legs tangled up in the climbing rope, his left arm wedged at his side, and buried up to his neck in snow. Apart from his head and right arm being free, he was unable to move.

Looking up to see how he might escape, he was horrified to see two blocks of ice hurtling toward him. He knew he was about to die. But just before the blocks reached him, they wedged between the walls of the crevasse, forming a roof ten feet above his head and showering him with debris. He was buried alive, unable to move, and as far as he knew the only person to survive.

Not surprisingly, his initial reaction was sheer panic. But struggling to control his emotions, he started to think about survival. As he had fallen, he had lost his hat. He knew he would have to keep himself warm in that cold place. And he was aware that we lose most of our body heat through our heads. It would be essential to find some way of retaining that heat.

Searching around, he saw a red, expedition-issue hat lying in the snow nearby. Thinking it was his, with his free hand he reached over to pick it up. The next moment, as he lifted the hat out of the snow, he was amazed to see black hair where the hat had been. For the first time, he realized one of his companions was buried beside him.

Dave scraped the snow away from the face. Nima Tsering, whose lips were already turning blue, spat out snow and ice and started to breathe. As he saw where he was, he started to struggle and the two of them began fighting for their lives in a quicksand of shifting snow and ice.

Above them, Rusty Baillie heard a noise coming out of the ice beneath his feet. Finding an opening, he looked down and gasped. "My God! You're alive!" Quickly, he lowered a rope with an ice axe, enabling the two survivors to chop their way to safety.

Blair Griffiths had not been so lucky. He had been pinned between two blocks of ice and was killed instantly.

Blair was the cameraman. He was the guy who was going to bring our story into living rooms across North America. He was the only professional cameraman on the expedition.

On the walk in, I had hiked with Blair. We had developed a close friendship and shared a tent for three weeks. On the day before we reached Everest base camp, we had climbed up a ridge above Lobuche to get a better view of the mountain we had come so far to climb. The verdant grassy slope was resplendent with a spectacular display of alpine flowers. From the top, we had a magnificent view of Everest and its sister peaks.

That night, after Blair had come down off this idyllic hillside, he had written in his journal, "I don't want to die, but if the pale horse should decide to come along, there isn't a better cathedral to stay in." His ashes now lie scattered on that very spot.

For the second time in two days, we had to carry down a friend and a colleague. For the second time, we had to build a funeral pyre. In the simple ceremony that followed, expedition member Tim Auger read a poem he had composed:

> This is the way of all eternity:
> As we see him now, so shall we be.
> When the time comes to follow him
> To where the mountain wind blows,
> Go as he does, with a good heart.

After such an optimistic start to our climb, four people had died in two accidents in two days. Our bubble of invincibility had been burst forever.

At the time of the expedition, my daughter, Jillian, was five. Like everyone else back home, Peggy and Jillian had heard on the news that a Canadian climber had died, but the details were sketchy. Nobody knew who had been involved in the second accident. Friends and relatives started calling the house to find out if Peggy knew anything more. Exhausted by the constant anxiety, she took Jillian for a walk to get some fresh air. As they reached the bottom of our street, one of Jillian's little friends came running up to her shouting, "Jillian! Jillian! Did you hear your daddy's been killed on Mount Everest?"

Jillian stuck out her chin and gave him a look that was stoic. "No, he wasn't," she said with defiance. "He wouldn't do anything that silly. He loves his family too much." Then she took Peggy's hand and they continued walking together around the corner.

When I heard that story I was torn apart. I couldn't help wondering what she would have felt if I had been the one who had died. Would she have felt I didn't love her? I was not the one taking the risks on Everest. Peggy and Jillian were taking the real risks. It's easy to die. It is the ones who are left behind who have to pick up the pieces.

As soon as I heard Bill's message, I started the hike to base camp, but because of the distance and the steep climb, it took me two days to return. As I worked my way through the last moraine, I was desperately trying to figure out how to put this climb back together again. I felt a tremendous responsibility toward the sponsors, the people who had gone out on a limb to fund our expedition. After all, I was the one who had persuaded them to become involved.

As I was climbing a steep incline toward the village of Lobuche, I was surprised to see one of our climbers coming toward me down the trail.

"Have you heard what's happening up there?" he said. "It's complete chaos. The thing's falling apart." He told me that he and five other climbers, some of the best on the team, were leaving the expedition.

Continuing on my way, I met the others, one by one. Each had a different perspective and a different story to tell. They seemed to be drifting off without any clear reason. The expedition seemed to be collapsing. I thought, if we're going to abandon the climb, for God's sake let's do it together, not in dribs and drabs.

By the time I reached base camp, I had made a decision. Walking into the crowded kitchen tent, I went right up to Bill March. I told him that I thought we should abandon the expedition to minimize bad publicity, and that the entire team should withdraw in good grace.

That really set the cat among the pigeons!

I realize now that I had spoken in haste before hearing the other side of the story. For the previous two days, the remainder of the team had been trying to pull the pieces together again. Now, some of the team members saw me attempting to destroy all they had been trying to rebuild. That night, nobody had much sleep. Lying awake in my tent, I could hear the others talking.

The next morning, I felt sheepish and awkward as I walked into the kitchen tent. Bill and a group of climbers were talking intently. He motioned me over and laid out a plan to change the route from the unclimbed south spur that we had

From The Edmonton Sun, *September 10, 1982.*

hoped to pioneer to the less technically demanding South Col route. This was the classic approach first completed by Sir Edmund Hillary's expedition in 1953.

The thinking was that the South Col route could be managed with a smaller team, which would make it possible to move more quickly through the danger zones. Because we already had some equipment in place at Camp I, we would only have to pass through the Icefall once on the way up and once more coming down, when the climb was over. The plan made a lot of sense, and I saw immediately that we could still achieve our goal of reaching Everest's summit while minimizing the risk. We could still make our country and our sponsors proud.

But there was a problem. We had six guys hiking back to Kathmandu who had left the expedition in haste and who all had different stories to tell. The media were going to meet them separately, and the resulting confusion might blow the expedition apart. I was worried about more than just the sponsors and our families. False reports criticizing the expedition would be bad for the morale of those who remained, and the team effort would suffer. In addition, our radio at base camp was still not fully operational. To get news out we had to rely on Sherpas running back and forth along the 150-mile long trail. It could take several days to get a message to Kathmandu.

But a solution was at hand. That very day, we heard that a helicopter was flying in from Kathmandu with a television cameraman aboard. It was decided that I would fly to Kathmandu for a few days and tell the story of what had happened. I could then return to base camp, reacclimatize my body to the rarefied air and join the team for the push up the mountain.

Success seems to be mainly a question of hanging on when others have let go.

—Unknown

SEVEN

THE OTHER SIDE OF EVEREST

Over and above all else, the story of mountaineering is a story of
faith and affirmation; that the high road is the good road; that
there are still among us those who are willing to struggle and suffer
greatly for wholly ideal ends; that security is not the be-all and end-
all of living; that there are conquests to be won in the world other
than over our fellow man. The climbing of earth's heights, in itself,
means little. That men and women want and try to climb them
means everything. For it is the ultimate wisdom of the mountains
that {we are never so much human} as when we are striving for
what is beyond our grasp, and that there is no battle worth the
winning save that against our own ignorance and fear.
—James Ramsay Ullman

W HEN I ARRIVED IN
Kathmandu, I took a taxi straight to the expedition headquar-
ters at the Everest Sheraton Hotel and ran into a media storm.
I was straight off Everest, still wearing my climbing gear,
looking dirty and disheveled. I had lost a lot of weight and
was gaunt and hollow-eyed. At first, nobody recognized me.
I walked right by a swarm of journalists waiting in the lobby.
But soon I found myself blinking into a TV camera, answering
faint questions as they buzzed from satellite to satellite across
tens of thousands of miles into a tiny earphone.

Struggling for composure, I reported to the millions of viewers in North America: "It's been a very emotional time, as you can imagine. Four people have been killed during our expedition on Mount Everest within two days. We have been through a heartrending time trying to reach a decision on whether to abandon our expedition or whether to proceed. I think now that we've reached the decision to proceed, we're all very relieved and are focusing our intentions on continuing.

"We will proceed and our objective is to proceed with the utmost caution. I'd like people back home to understand that we are not madmen, but that we are sensible human beings and we will only proceed with great caution. We will take our time. We will wait for the very best weather. We will go through dangerous sections very quickly and limit the number of times we are exposed to danger and hope that by utilizing these principles we'll be able to climb the mountain safely from this point."

My focus in going to Kathmandu was to protect the interests of the climbing team and to give the public an accurate picture of what had happened on the mountain. I wanted to make sure the media were getting the facts straight. Looking for controversy, they had already started to focus on the guys who had left the expedition, calling them defectors, traitors, deserters. But in my opinion, these men were heroes, and I said so. They had their own reasons for leaving—sincere, personal reasons. The climbers who left had been intimately involved with the accidents. Some of them had been buried in the avalanche and near death themselves. Others had been there to see their friends die. They all had families to think about.

A media juggernaut had moved into Kathmandu. The entire top floor of the Everest Sheraton had been turned into a television studio. Millions of dollars of state-of-the-art communications equipment had been flown in to replace the furniture. A satellite dish was located outside the hotel, beaming signals into space. CanEverEx, our promotional arm, had flown in two one-ton generators to guarantee the electrical power needed to send signals halfway around the world. Over the weeks to come, a microwave relay system was helicoptered into place, allowing us to conduct live interviews from North America with the guys on the mountain.

In addition to the Canadian CBC crew, which had been there from the start, the American ABC network had also sent in a television crew. There were five or six wire services represented and several national newspaper chains. It was total chaos. Nobody knew anything, and there was a huge demand for information.

It soon became evident to me that I was never going to be able to return to the climb because there was just too much need for a spokesperson in the media center in Kathmandu.

Distorted media headlines that were published in Canada prior to my arrival in Kathmandu.

There was nobody else available who could interpret the events on the mountain. I knew the guys on Everest wanted to try to pull things together and I knew they were worried about what people were saying.

Even before I arrived in Kathmandu, some negative articles had been printed in Canada. One extremely critical magazine story had built its case around thirty factual errors; the resulting anger of the climbing team was hard on our morale. Sensational headlines, like "Everest Assault Called a Mess," and misleading articles quoting people who had never even been to Everest and who had no personal knowledge of events were not likely to inspire much confidence in the public or in our sponsors' perceptions of our efforts.

Climbing Mount Everest is as much a psychological challenge as it is a physical one. You do not need any distractions. I realized my role had become a critical one, to protect the team by making sure that whatever was sent home was factual and accurate so the men on Everest could get on with their job of climbing the mountain.

The odd thing was that I had been concerned about media coverage well before the climb. I recall standing in the kitchen of our small cedar house in Canmore several weeks before I left for Nepal, asking Peggy, "What are we going to do if there's an accident on this mountain? We're going to be 150 miles away from Kathmandu. How are we going to be able to explain it?" Her reaction was, "If it happens, it happens, and you'll figure it out at the time."

Now I was struggling with the realization that I should stay in Kathmandu to deal with the confusion of the media. After the expedition team had departed from Canada, CanEverEx had signed a contract with CBC guaranteeing live television coverage from the mountain. This had never before been achieved on Everest, and the television producers were pressuring me to get on the radio and tell the climbers to carry the camera. I knew perfectly well they were not going to worry about a television camera at this point. Completing the climb safely was their one and only focus. I was caught in the middle, hearing the demands of the media on one side and wanting to protect the climbers' needs on the other.

I was hesitant to say too much, but when I talked to the guys on the radio, I would try to explain the difficult situation I was experiencing. Finally, the team leaders got together at base camp and told me they thought I should stay in Kathmandu. It was an incredible weight off my shoulders to know that they understood the importance of what I was doing.

So began my own personal Everest, the challenge of interpreting the event for the Canadian and American public. Sometimes I think I worked harder in Kathmandu than if I had stayed on the mountain. I was in the media center for more than a month, putting in an average of twenty hours a day. I didn't even leave the hotel for the first three weeks.

Every day would start with dragging myself out of bed at 5:00 a.m. to make a radio call to base camp while reception was still reasonably clear. Even at that early hour, however, I would usually have to strain to hear what was being said through the atmospheric interference. Base camp was 150 miles away and there were twenty-thousand-foot mountains in between. It would already be hot in Kathmandu, and I would sweat profusely as I struggled to decipher communications through the crackle and buzz. Reporters were always hovering over me, and I had to choose my words carefully.

By seven o'clock, I would have prepared a press release and before breakfast I would brief the wire service journalists from Associated Press, Canadian Press, United Press International, Reuters and others. This was followed by a press conference for other reporters who were following our progress.

Around ten o'clock, I would meet with radio journalists to prepare reports in both English and French, before their stories were beamed to North America.

One of these sessions was particularly challenging. Michel Lacroix, a French-Canadian journalist, wanted to

On the roof of the Everest Sheraton hotel.

interview me in French. I had studied French in school, but I am not fluent in the language. So Michel would ask me questions in English and I would write down my answers. He would then translate my answers into French and I would write them out phonetically. Then I would practice reading my answers over and over, with Michel coaching me on the proper pronunciation until I got it right. At that point, we would record an interview with me reading from my French script and he would send it to Canada by satellite.

My accent must have been a hit, because the very next day a radio station in Montreal called and asked me to do a live open-line radio show in French. Needless to say, I politely declined.

For the rest of the day, I would work with the CBC and ABC television crews, either giving interviews or helping edit the day's report, checking everything for accuracy. Often, we would work right through lunch and dinner and sometimes until well after midnight.

As part of this process, I was asked to do a series of "live" interviews on CBC national television with Barbara Frum, a highly respected Canadian journalist with the nightly news magazine, *The Journal*. There I was, sitting in a hotel room in Kathmandu with flies buzzing around my head and an earphone plugged in my ear while I stared into a camera lens and tried to answer Barbara Frum's faint questions from half a world away. It was intimidating, to say the least. She was used to interviewing celebrities and world leaders, and had a reputation as a hard-nosed, no-nonsense journalist. As it turned out, she only wanted to cut through the rumors and get straight to the facts. She later told me that the Everest story was one of the highlights of her journalism career.

The ABC television crew was reporting for the *Nightline* program in the United States, which was interested in our story because ours was the first expedition to be covered live from the mountain. On a couple of occasions, I participated in lengthy interviews with Ted Koppel, linking, via satellite, Kathmandu with high-altitude doctor Peter Hackett in Anchorage and Rusty Baillie in Calgary.

I would usually collapse into bed around one o'clock in the morning to get some much-needed sleep before starting all over again. However, it was not unusual for my phone to start ringing a couple of hours later with an interview request from a journalist in Canada who, because of the time difference, had just arrived at work.

Included in our communications system was a dedicated telephone link from Kathmandu to North America. Incredibly, I could sit on the closed toilet seat of the expedition's media center, the bathroom having been converted into a functional sound studio, dial the number nine and find myself speaking to an operator in the Montreal exchange. From there, it was a simple matter of dialing an area code and local number, and I could communicate with anyone throughout the continent. Given the rather elementary state of telecommunications in Nepal at the time (we had even shipped in our own telephones from Canada), this was a vivid demonstration of the evolving power of satellite communications in our increasingly globalized society.

To send our news stories to Canada required bouncing signals off three satellites rotating in geosynchronous orbit more than twenty-two thousand miles above the equator. From the earth station we had positioned outside the Everest Sheraton in Kathmandu, the signal would beam up to a satellite over the Indian Ocean and be reflected down to a receiving station in the United Kingdom. From there, it would be retransmitted to a second satellite over the Atlantic Ocean and directed to an earth station in Nova Scotia. Finally, the signal was sent to Anik, the Canadian domestic satellite, where it would be deflected into TV sets across the country. In total, the signal would travel more than 133,000 miles each way and more than a quarter of a million miles through space—and it would take less than one second for the entire two-way transmission to occur!

In the final analysis, the effort paid off in spades. Public awareness of our expedition was the highest in Everest's climbing history. CBC television gave the story twenty hours of detailed news coverage and it was featured twice on ABC's *Nightline* with Ted Koppel. On our return, a one-hour television special rated an unheard-of 80 percent on the entertainment index. In addition, the climb was the subject of over three thousand newspaper and magazine articles worldwide. A survey afterward indicated that three out of four people in Canada had followed the climb with interest.

The support from back home was incredible. I will never forget receiving big brown envelopes full of letters from elementary schools across Canada with barely legible words scribbled on them. Neither will I forget those sketches of pyramid-shaped mountains crowned with big red-and-white flags streaming from the summit and little spider figures hanging from the sides of vertical precipices with scribbled words at the bottom of a page saying: "Keep going. We're with you. Jason, Grade 1, Toronto."

We were climbing the mountain for all of those people. They had become a part of our team.

Working as a team, you can overcome unbelievable odds and achieve things that others believe to be impossible.

—*Mike Beedell*

EIGHT

ON TOP OF THE WORLD

*Nobody can fight their way to the top, and stay at the top, without
exercising the fullest measure of grit, courage, determination, and
resolution. Everybody who gets anywhere does so because they are
firstly resolved to progress in this world and then have enough
"stick-to-itiveness" to transform their resolution into reality.
Without resolution, nobody can win any worthwhile place among
their fellow men.*

—B.C. Forbes

BACK ON THE MOUNTAIN,
a month and a day after we had arrived at base camp, a team of
eight climbers and sixteen Sherpas pushed up to reestablish
and stock Camp I. They had all made one final harrowing carry
through the Icefall before closing it. Bill March, the team
leader, broke his own rule of one carry per climber and went
back and forth three times in order to demonstrate his commitment and to help rebuild the Sherpas' confidence in our
expedition.

Climbing progressed smoothly and quickly above
Camp I. But it was never easy. As they climbed higher and
higher, the men were pushing further and further into the rarefied air. With a smaller team, they did not have enough man-
power to carry a full supply of heavy oxygen cylinders. All the

way up to the final camp at 26,200 feet, the party was struggling to breathe natural air, and only above that height would they use bottled oxygen. Soon, everyone was exhausted.

Suffering from oxygen deficiency, lack of sleep, dehydration, extreme sunburn, snow blindness and unimaginable stress, the climbers were in a race against deteriorating weather as winter approached. With extreme effort, they finally pushed up to Camp III at 23,000 feet, but the jet-stream winds were blasting at more than one hundred miles an hour across the summit ridge, and the lead climbers were forced back to Camp II.

The advance party was so exhausted they started to think about taking a time out—retreating all the way to base camp to spend a couple of weeks recovering in the denser air. Then they hoped to be strong enough to return to their high point and launch one last push for the summit.

Sherpas climbing Lhotse face of Everest.

It was at that point that the Sherpas stepped forward. They knew from their vast experience that if we retreated to base camp, it would be unlikely we would have the strength to climb up again. So, without having to be asked, they offered to take the load off our shoulders and push ahead themselves.

We had finally become a team. We were no longer a group of men from the West working with a group of men from the East. Our relationship was no longer that of Canadian employers and Nepalese employees. This was a team that had shared adversity together, had learned to respect and trust each other and who now wanted to go all the way to the summit together.

The next morning the Sherpas pushed ahead. In one amazing day, they climbed from Camp II to the final camp on the South Col, 4,500 feet up the exposed Lhotse Face of Mount Everest without breathing oxygen from bottles and carrying double loads of more than one hundred pounds on their backs. In that one day of effort, they opened the door to the summit. The very next day, the weather improved dramatically. The winds that had raked the peak for weeks, blowing a plume of snow for more than two miles into Tibet, suddenly disappeared. The jet stream had moved up into the atmosphere above the peak. We had perfect conditions to go all the way.

Laurie Skreslet was the person we chose to represent us on the top. He was to be accompanied by Sungdare and Lhakpa Dorje, two of our strongest Sherpas.

In the early days of the climb, Laurie had fallen and injured his ribs. In fact, he thought he might have broken a rib. Recognizing that he would heal faster at lower elevation, our expedition doctors had sent him down to a hospital at twelve thousand feet for medical treatment. He was there for several days, resting, breathing the denser air and getting stronger every day.

Meanwhile, the other members of the expedition were pushing forward above twenty thousand feet, getting weaker and weaker from lack of oxygen. When Laurie rejoined the

Camp IV on the South Col.

Above South Col, climbing towards the south summit of Everest.

climbing party, he was clearly the strongest member of the team. Because of this, we asked him to go to the summit to maximize the chances of success for the whole expedition.

On October 4, 1982, Laurie Skreslet, Sungdare and Lhakpa Dorje spent the night poised in their tents at Camp IV. Down in Kathmandu, I was too excited to sleep. The entire media crew was camped out on the floor of the media center awaiting news from the mountain. The tension was unbearable.

The following morning at 4:15, with the temperature near −30°F, the three turned on their oxygen sets and, by the glow of their headlamps, began climbing smooth green ice above the South Col. Soon, however, they found themselves breaking through the crust, punching post holes into the underlying snow. Even with the benefit of bottled oxygen, the going was extremely tough and dictated a rest after every five steps. Then they would push themselves for the next five minutes, the next few steps . . .

"The climbing," Skreslet recalls, "was surprisingly demanding. Put on a snowmobile suit, big boots, heavy mitts, a face mask, steamed-up goggles, a toque that slides down over your eyes and a forty-pound pack on your back, then have someone knock the wind out of you and see if you can climb your own back fence. It was enough just to figure out where to put my feet. There were so many things that could go wrong— we were so extended—that it was just one step at a time, one step higher."

Shortly after 12:30 p.m. on October 5, I was called to the radio to receive a message from base camp. The words crackled into my headphones:

"We made it! We made it!"

I was absolutely ecstatic. I was on top of the world. The whole newsroom, the entire hotel, rocked with cheers and elation. Traditionally jaded journalists hugged and slapped hands. I could feel tears streaming down my face. I had absolutely no regret that I wasn't there on the summit because I knew I had done my job, just as Laurie had done his. I was as proud as he was. In fact, I was probably prouder because I had invested so much effort in this project over all those years.

. Immediately, tributes began to pour into the media center in Kathmandu. Canadian Prime Minister Pierre Trudeau sent a telegram congratulating the team for "a remarkable achievement. Your heroic struggle to set foot on the highest point on earth has captured the imagination of all Canadians and the attention of the world. Throughout your long and dangerous climb, our hopes and prayers were with you."

When you see one person standing on top of Everest, or achieving any worthwhile goal in life, it is important to recognize the contribution of all the people who put them there.

On the summit of Everest, Laurie took pictures of everything in sight—the mountains, the panorama, the Sherpas who were with him. Then he decided it was time to get a picture of himself. To his surprise, he discovered he had run out of film. Searching around in his pack, he remembered he had not thought of carrying spare film in the rush to leave the tents that morning. Shaking his head, he realized he would not get a picture of himself on the summit!

Obviously, he was disappointed. All of us would love to have that picture, with the flag streaming into the wind from the top of the world—the one that would grace the front cover of *Time* or *Life* magazines. But when you think about it, pictures aren't that important. You learn nothing about the background or the struggle from looking at a picture. In fact, you don't learn much while standing on the top of Mount Everest. The learning takes place when you come down and have the time to reflect upon the journey, upon the struggle that got you to that point of achievement.

For Sungdare, the expedition's strongest Sherpa, this ascent to Everest's peak was his third success on the mountain. He was a quiet, handsome man of twenty-five. His climbing career had started nine years previously when he was a mail runner for a Japanese expedition. In 1975, he had been hired by Chris Bonington's British expedition and reached Camp V on Everest's extremely difficult southwest face. In 1979, he had summitted for the first time with a West German team, accompanying Hannelore Schmatz and the American Ray Genet to the top. Hannelore was the fourth woman to climb the world's highest mountain.

On the way down in 1979, Sungdare's companions had collapsed from exhaustion and were forced to spend the night out without oxygen at twenty-eight thousand feet. During that night, with no protection from the wind and the cold, Genet succumbed to hypothermia and died. Next morning, with Hannelore still alive but unable to move, Sungdare descended to the South Col and returned with more oxygen. But when this ran out, she, too, collapsed and died. Returning alone, Sungdare discovered he had frostbite and subsequently had to have toes amputated from both feet.

It took him a long time to walk again. He had to wear special boots. But he returned to Everest in 1981 and reached the summit for a second time with an American medical research expedition. With our team, he became the first man to climb the world's highest peak three times. He drowned in 1989 in the Dudh Kosi river near his home below the mountain he loved.

Sungdare was a national hero in Nepal, not only because he had reached the peak of Everest so often, but because of that incredible example he gave us all, of picking himself up off the floor when he lost his toes and climbing onto the mountaintop. On my return hike to Everest from Namche Bazar, when I had heard news of the second accident, I had met Sungdare on the trail and walked with him for several hours as we approached base camp. During our conversation, I asked him why he kept returning to Everest time and again. His answer was very deceptive. He said, "I climb the mountain to see once again what the view is like from the top."

Clearly we cannot stand forever on the summit. There will always be times when we are down in the valley. But it is the memory of what it was like on the mountaintop that gives us the inspiration to climb out of those valleys where we meet the adversity that will continue to challenge us throughout our lives.

The expedition, however, was not yet over. As long as the weather stayed clear, there were other climbers who wanted to try for the peak. Two days later, on October 7, Pat Morrow, Pema Dorje and Lhakpa Tshering also reached the top of the world. Of the group who stayed on after the tragedies, six were able to make it all the way to the summit.

A professional adventure photographer by vocation, Pat painstakingly shot exposure after exposure, clearly capturing the curvature of the earth's crust as the mountains blended into the high plateau of Tibet off in the distance. Visibility was easily one hundred miles in every direction. In his subsequent book, *Beyond Everest: Quest for the Seven Summits*, Pat commented: "It was as though we were in a hot-air balloon, peering down on the tops of the cumulus clouds two miles below. It was, quite simply, one of the most spectacular places I've been."

For Pema Dorje, this was his first time to Everest's summit. More amazingly, Everest was the first mountain he had ever climbed. We met him when he had been hired as a base camp cook during our training climb of 24,688-foot Annapurna IV the previous winter. He had impressed us with his strength and dedication, and we had invited him to join the Sherpa team for the Everest climb. He followed Pat Morrow all the way to the top!

Many people have since been tempted to ask what is left for this young man, who climbed the world's highest mountain on his first attempt. Well, of course, everything is left. His challenge is to digest the Everest experience, learn the lessons and then move on to fresh challenges.

In 1992, on the tenth anniversary of our climb, I returned to Nepal with Peggy and Jillian to hike once more

View from the top of the world.

Pema Dorje and Lhakpa Tshering on the summit.

to the base of Everest and to revisit those incredible Sherpa people who had been so critical to our success. While there, we met Pema Dorje, who is now in great demand as a well-paid trekking and climbing leader for commercial groups. He was smartly dressed in color-coordinated clothing, wearing stylish Vuarnet sunglasses and a white hat. He looked every inch a traditional European mountain guide. Truly he had digested the experience and learned the lessons.

When I look back on the Everest story today, I realize there was nothing exceptional about the people who shared in this experience. We were just a group of average people in pursuit of a goal—a goal that we had chosen out of a recognition of our strengths as mountaineers, but also out of an acceptance of our limitations. We set out to build a team where the strengths of one group would offset the limitations of the other. It was this team that climbed Everest during one of the most arduous seasons in recent memory.

We faced death, deterioration and despondency on Everest. We were forced to dig deep. In the process, we discovered we were capable of more than we had ever thought possible: that we had the resources to keep going no matter what the obstacles.

Life is a series of ups and downs, from valleys to peaks and back down again. We attain goals, we suffer setbacks. The art, I think, is to remember what we felt on the heights when we are down in the valleys.

The lessons of Everest are lessons for us all—challenging, preparing, working as a team, treating people as equals, adapting to changing conditions, facing inner fears, setting goals that stretch, learning from setbacks, recognizing the need for support and remaining open to the next horizon, and the next, and the next.

Putting these events into context, however, it is important to realize that Mount Everest was just one arena where a group of dedicated, adventurous people chose to pursue their dreams.

The Everest climbers in Kathmandu after the climb.

We all live in different arenas and each of us has the power to be just as adventurous in our own situation. We are all climbers. We all have our impossible dreams. We all have the potential to stand proudly on the summit of our lives.

Achievement cannot be a pinnacle. It is a plateau that is a sustainable high, something that is constant and not a lot of ups and downs.

—*Pat Morrow*

NINE

GOING ONE STEP BEYOND

*I find the great thing in this world is not so much where you stand,
as in what direction you are moving. To reach the port of heaven you
must sometimes sail with the wind, and sometimes against it. But
you must sail, and not drift, nor lie at anchor.*

—Oliver Wendell Holmes

WHEN THE EVEREST TEAM
arrived in Canada in late October 1982, I had been away from
home for more than one hundred days. In the year prior to our
departure, I had resigned from my job at the Banff Centre to
work full-time on expedition organization. Now I was unemployed. In preparing for the Everest challenge, there had been
no time to consider what might happen afterward. There had
only been enough energy to focus on the job at hand. Now I
had to find work to support Peggy and Jillian, who had struggled so valiantly to keep things going in my absence so I could
have a place to come back to, to sleep in safety, after the climb
was over.

The urgent challenge was to pay off our expedition
debt, which we had been unable to fund before the climb.
Almost immediately the phone started to ring. Because of the
high profile of the Everest story—it was covered daily on
national television for more than a month—interest was

113

high. Having watched our dramatic life-and-death struggles, corporate executives and the general public alike wanted to hear our story. They clearly saw the analogy between what it took to climb the world's highest mountain and the principles that can lead to personal and professional success in everyday life.

We were immediately sucked into a whirlwind of public appearances across North America. Having been appointed as managing director of CanEverEx Inc., the expedition's promotional arm, I was forced to establish an office with four people working full-time to meet the demand. In the first year after our return, we scheduled more than five hundred appearances and presentations, in which all the climbing team took part. One day, we had five climbers speaking in five different cities across the country. To recognize and thank our sponsors, a traveling exhibit was created and displayed at shopping centers and in major trade shows and exhibitions from coast to coast.

At the end of the year, we were debt-free and able for the first time to consider what the future might hold after Everest.

Having participated in such a powerful experience, however, it was clear to me that I could never again be the same person. All my instincts told me that I must move on, take the Everest experience, learn from it and set new goals, higher mountains to climb. But what was that next challenge to involve?

One memorable day, having returned from lunching with Canada's then Prime Minister Pierre Elliott Trudeau, and being introduced in the House of Commons in Ottawa, the home of Canada's government, I recall discussing the future with Peggy. In one innocent but insightful comment she said, "Well you've finally climbed Everest after seventeen years of dreaming about it. Now it's time to go one step beyond Everest." A lightbulb flashed in my mind! We would form a company called One Step Beyond to take the Everest story and apply it to helping others climb their own metaphorical mountains in their business and professional lives.

To progress in life, you must constantly be climbing new moun-tains and seeking out new adventures.

Since that day, I have never looked back. While the presence of rugged mountains is still very important to me—Peggy, Jillian and I remain in our cedar home in the small town of Canmore, Alberta, in the Canadian Rockies—the mountains I am now climbing are entrepreneurial. From Canmore I travel widely, spending more than two hundred days a year flying from city to city, from country to country around the world. The challenge is one of communication, to instill in my audiences the thrill of adventure and to articulate a philosophy that will help others climb their own mountains of change in these difficult times.

It is a message of universal impact. Everyone can reflect on the analogies of my keynote presentation, called *Climbing Your Own Everest: What It Takes To Get To The Top* or my half-day seminar *Meeting the Challenge of Change*. To date, I have addressed more than half a million people from more than a thousand major corporations and professional associa-tions in twenty countries worldwide. In one recent two-month period, I spoke to audiences in Singapore, Malaysia, Australia, Hong Kong, China, Greece, Mexico, Canada and the United States.

But the quest for adventure remains deep within me.

Seven years after Everest, I helped to initiate an ambi-tious five-year project to commemorate and reenact the expe-ditions of Sir Alexander Mackenzie who, in the latter years of the eighteenth century, was the first to travel by land across the North American continent from the Atlantic to the Arctic and Pacific oceans. A Scotsman by birth and a fur trader by profes-sion, Mackenzie made his journeys on foot and in birchbark canoes paddled by French-Canadian voyageurs and with the guidance of the indigenous people he met along the way.

Motivated by a desire to discover the Northwest Passage, which would facilitate transAtlantic trade between Europe and Asia, his voyages opened up vast unknown territories to development by the fur trade. Perhaps more important, he was the first to link Canada as a nation from sea to sea to sea, traveling from Montreal to the Arctic Ocean in 1789, and on to Bella Coola, British Columbia, on the Pacific coast of Canada, in 1792–1793.

In his landmark book, *Caesars of the Wilderness*, one of a trilogy on the history of the fur trade in North America, author and historian Peter C. Newman comments: "Alexander Mackenzie is a legitimate Canadian hero. . . . [His] physical feat of having been the first white man to take an expedition across the upper continent—thirteen years before Meriwether Lewis and William Clark led a much larger and better-equipped force to the more southerly American shore of the Pacific—overshadowed his considerable contributions to the politics of the fur-trade, to international diplomacy, and to Arctic literature."

It is an unfortunate fact that today more is known of the Lewis and Clark expeditions across the central United States, even though they were initiated by President Thomas Jefferson only after Jefferson had read Mackenzie's journals, published during Mackenzie's retirement in Scotland in 1801.

The Sir Alexander Mackenzie Canada Sea-to-Sea Bicentennial Expedition was launched under the honorary patronage of HRH Prince Andrew, Duke of York, in an attempt to correct this omission. On the two hundredth anniversary of Mackenzie's original explorations, Dr. Jim Smithers of Lakehead University and I linked up in an effort to educate young Canadians about the historical importance of this man and the early European explorers in whose footsteps he followed: Cabot, Cartier, Champlain, La Vérendrye, Boucher de Niverville and others. By drawing an analogy between Canada's adventurous heritage and the changing world of today, we hoped to make a statement about the role the spirit of adventure must play in our modern industrial society.

The Canada Sea-to-Sea canoe brigade descending the Mackenzie River.

Having made a three-week reconnaissance in an inflatable Zodiac the previous summer, in 1989 I joined the outdoor recreation students from Lakehead University as they paddled replicas of fur-trade canoes for 2,160 miles from Fort McMurray in northern Alberta across Lake Athabasca (the fifth largest lake in North America) and down the Mackenzie River to Kendall Island in the Arctic Ocean. Dressed in traditional clothing from the days of the fur trade, the students spent fifty-one days on the water, made more than two million paddle strokes and battled hordes of mosquitoes, learning firsthand of the incredible hardships endured by Mackenzie's expedition. At twelve communities along the way, they performed a historical pageant before thousands of people, giving the residents of Canada's north an unforgettable window into their adventurous past.

During the summer months from 1991 to 1993, these modern voyageurs completed the Canada Sea-to-Sea project by paddling 5,490 miles across Canada, starting in the Atlantic waters of the St. Lawrence River near Montreal and ending at Bella Coola, on the Pacific coast of British Columbia. Two hundred years to the day after he had first reached that spot, the students returned to the very rock in the Dean Channel where Alexander Mackenzie had written in melted grease mixed with vermilion: "Alex Mackenzie from Canada by land 22d July 1793." Today, the Canadian coat of arms bears the inscription *A Mari Usque Ad Mare*, the Latin phrase denoting that Canada is a nation that stretches "from sea to sea," thanks in large part to the adventurous spirit of this extraordinary man and others like him.

To a considerable degree, Mackenzie attained his goals because of his amazing ability to embrace the new world he explored, flexibly adapting to every situation in which he found himself. Born on the island of Lewis off the west coast of Scotland, he left behind his Scottish ways when he arrived in North America, embracing the Native life-style (their canoes, clothing, and food) as he pushed relentlessly into the unknown. He led by example, constantly looking for any new knowledge that might enhance his chances of success. He made his journeys across tens of thousands of miles of uncharted territory without a single loss of life, safely returning all of his men to their families in Montreal at the end of his expeditions.

In our North American heritage, we have examples of other pioneers who were not so flexible or so open-minded.

In May 1845, some fifty-two years after Mackenzie had completed his journey to the Pacific, another expedition set out from British shores to continue the search for the Northwest Passage, a long-sought-after sea route through the arctic islands of North America to the Pacific. The expedition was under the command of Sir John Franklin, a distinguished fifty-nine-year-old veteran of many previous arctic campaigns, and included 129 men sailing two of the finest ships of the time, the *Terror* and the *Erebus*. They were described in the London press as the pride of the British naval and merchant fleets.

However, the expedition proved unsuited to the arctic challenge. Crossing the Atlantic Ocean, they rounded the southern tip of Greenland, entered the icebound waters of Lancaster Sound in northern Canada and sailed off the map. Pushing westward, they were soon trapped by the ice pack and for two winters were forced to drift with the currents. Finally, the boats were crushed and started to sink. Isolated, they found themselves without transportation hundreds of miles from the nearest fur-trading posts on the shores of Hudson Bay to the south.

It is what happened at this point that gives us pause for thought as we struggle to adapt to the rapidly changing world in which we live today.

Forced to contemplate the realities of survival in this hostile world, the sailors unloaded their ships of all the essentials, piling their large sleds high with equipment and food. Onto other sleds, they loaded lifeboats, filled them with goods and started hauling the sleds southward toward safety. Subsequently, all 129 brave souls disappeared from the face of the earth.

". . . a boat mounted on a sledge . . . " A painting of the remains of the Franklin expedition.

For the next ten years, numerous expeditions were sent out from London and New York in attempts to discover what had happened to Franklin's expedition. It was by this process that the remaining uncharted coastline of arctic North America was mapped.

Finally, in May 1859, an expedition financed by Lady Franklin and led by Captain Leopold M'Clintock came upon the skeleton of a young man. Near his body they found a clothes brush and a pocket comb. A few days later, the party discovered a cairn in which was a note indicating that the *Terror* and the *Erebus* had been abandoned on April 22, 1848. The same note related that Franklin had died of natural causes a year previously.

On May 30, 1859, the party found another amazing relic that was described in Vilhjalmur Stefansson's book *Unsolved Mysteries of the Arctic* as follows: ". . . a boat mounted on a sledge, a total weight of fourteen hundred pounds. A quantity of tattered clothing was lying inside, as also were two skeletons, one of them wrapped in clothes and furs. Five watches and two double-barreled guns were also found. There were five or six small books, most of them religious; silk handkerchiefs, towels, soap, sponge, toothbrush, hair combs, twine, nails, saws, files, bristles, wax ends, powder, shot, cartridges, knives. . . . " In short, as M'Clintock puts it, the crew was hauling ". . . a quantity of articles of one description and another truly astonishing in variety and such [that] modern sledge travelers in these regions would consider a mere accumulation of dead weight . . . and very likely to break down the strength of the sledge crews."

There was more: ". . . a multitude of footwear from sea boots to strong shoes, formal naval uniforms, a cigar case, dinner cutlery, twenty-six pieces of silver plate with the coat-of-arms of the senior officers . . . " all items that might have been of importance to civilized nineteenth-century travelers, but none of which was vital for survival in the icy conditions of the

Canadian Arctic in which members of the Franklin expedition had been forced to struggle for their lives.

In recent years, anthropologists have unearthed the frozen remains of seamen who had perished earlier in the Franklin expedition and have identified lead poisoning as a contributing factor to this tragedy. For the first time in exploration history, the Franklin sailors had been provisioned with food in tins—tins that had been soldered shut with a lead alloy. Lead must have leached into the food and from thence into their tissues, which quite likely contributed to irrational behavior during their struggle for survival.

At the same time, it appears clear that the inability of Franklin's officers to alter their perceptions of how British gentlemen must behave and live was a root cause of the tragedy. They had attempted to survive in the Arctic with the same formal traditions they would have enforced in London, and had exhausted themselves hauling heavy loads of useless material across the frozen tundra, dying in their tracks.

The question we must all ask ourselves today is this: Do we want to follow in the footsteps of Alexander Mackenzie or those of John Franklin? Should we open up our minds and embrace the realities of today's world, or do we complacently continue to cling to the comfortable perceptions and traditions of the past? The choice is ours to make and will ultimately dictate the outcome of our lives.

The study of such adventures is part of my ongoing desire to reflect upon our past, to attempt to put myself in the footsteps of the great explorers and to learn the lessons of our heritage. Truly, if we don't learn the lessons of history, we will never know how we might do better in the future.

As the pace of change increases, the spirit of adventure becomes more and more relevant in meeting the challenges of daily life. Today, more than ever before, we must acknowledge that there are no guarantees and that we face uncertainty at every step. The results of our struggles are unpredictable.

No one can say exactly what will happen tomorrow, next month or next year. In this context, life is a leap of faith. But, just as on the Troll Wall or on Everest, there is no benefit to worrying about what lies ahead. We cannot become consumed by the fear of what might be. We must move ahead with confidence, meet the challenge with optimism and discover within ourselves the ability to succeed.

More than five hundred years ago, when Columbus set out from Europe to head west across his own ocean of uncertainty, he had no accurate idea of where he was going. But he went anyway! His greatest asset was perhaps his persistence in the pursuit of his own new world of opportunity across the waters. He once wrote, "I plow ahead, no matter how the winds might lash me." This is a simple approach that is just as applicable to sailing across the unpredictable waters of today's world.

We all have within us the ability to be adventurous because we are descended from adventurous people. Everyone in modern society carries genes from predecessors who decades, perhaps centuries ago left behind the known world of the homeland and set out across uncharted waters to an uncertain future. In the process of plowing ahead, they found the curiosity to seek new opportunities, the courage to overcome fear of the unknown, the commitment to keep going through adversity, the creativity to adapt to changing conditions and the cooperation and communication needed to support each other in pursuit of common goals. Finally, they had the concentration that enabled them to keep focused on their goals despite all the distractions along the way.

In this process of personal discovery, our progenitors built a society of great sophistication. In this society, we have come to believe that security is assured and that life can be led without risk. It is a comfortable existence that we complacently accept as the norm and which we arrogantly assume will continue. But it is a world that, like it or not, we are being forced to leave behind as we face the challenges of the next millennium.

It is one of the great paradoxes of human existence that by our very nature we seek out comfort and predictability, using all our financial resources and intellectual powers to devise technologies that make our lives easier and less stressful. The paradox lies in that once we have created the comfort we desire, we must leave it all behind if we are to move forward in life.

In life, there is only one choice! We can try to stay where we are today, enjoying the security of the known world that we have conquered through our previous efforts. Or we can actively move ahead to meet the challenges of the future.

It is impossible to stay where we are! If we become complacent and stagnate, or start to drift, we will be left behind by more aggressive people. So the choice we must face today is this: Do we want to drift aimlessly, or do we want to leap forward into the unknown? There is no other choice! As William Jennings Bryan once wrote, "Destiny is not a matter of chance; it is a matter of choice. It is not something to be waited for; but rather something to be achieved."

What makes this difficult to appreciate is the growing lack of personal accountability that is widespread in modern society. Today, we seem not to want to be responsible for ourselves anymore. When we get into trouble, we look to the government to bail us out, or we try to claim on an insurance policy. Often the immediate reaction when faced with a challenging situation is to look for someone to blame, or somebody to sue. But this is not nature's way, and we are a part of the natural system, even if our every action seems to deny it. How often do we seem intent on destroying the natural environment that nurtures our life on earth?

The famous American author and lecturer Helen Keller, who was deaf and blind throughout her life, wrote: "Security is mostly a superstition. It does not exist in nature, nor do the children of man as a whole experience it. Avoiding danger is no safer in the long run than outright exposure. Life is either a daring adventure, or nothing!"

Hundreds of years before her, the famous French explorer Samuel de Champlain, who explored vast regions of the Great Lakes system in North America, wrote: "The advice I give to all adventurers is to seek a place where they may sleep in safety." This defines what I believe is the only real security we need in our lives.

In effect, security can only be found within ourselves, in our ability to apply all of our physical and mental resources to confront adversity and create from our efforts the results that we desire in our lives. While we need to work cooperatively with others to achieve common goals in the coming millennium, it is upon ourselves, and ourselves alone, that we can ultimately rely. To make the most of the opportunities that change creates, it will be vital that we understand the Adventure Attitude and learn to apply it in every aspect of our lives.

In order to achieve, the first thing one must have is a boundless spirit and a fortitude that never backs down. Then, you have to believe in yourself.

—*Mike Beedell*

TEN

THE NINE KEYS TO SUCCESS

Man alone, of all the creatures of earth, can change his own pattern.
Man alone is architect of his destiny. The greatest revolution in our
generation is the discovery that human beings, by changing the inner
attitudes of their minds, can change the outer aspects of their lives.
— *William James*

STATED SIMPLY, THE
Adventure Attitude is a paradigm through which we can see
the challenge of change with optimism and start to seek out
the opportunities that change creates.

All too often we see change as a threat, as something to
be feared. We are so consumed with the need for certainty and
predictability that we fail to accept that change is the only real
constant in our lives. As a result, we often don't seek the opportunities that change creates until we are forced to change by
some external influence beyond our control, be it economic cri-
sis, political realignment or personal tragedy.

This was certainly the case on Everest, when we were
forced to confront tragedy so early in the climb. We had to
accept the inevitability of those deaths. We had not caused
them by our own negligence; we had simply been in the
wrong place at the wrong time. But there were lessons to be
learned.

In fact, as we struggled to pull the expedition together in the aftermath of the tragedies, we started to question whether we had been trying to climb Everest the wrong way in the first place. We began to think that we had spent five years preparing for our expedition in the comfort of our homes, building a plan that was based upon a series of assumptions about what it would be like on a mountain half a world away. When we arrived at the base of Everest, we had not checked to see if the assumptions were correct. We had assumed they were correct and become complacent, developing a tunnel vision that prevented us from looking around us, from seeing what was going on around us on the mountain. Because of this, we had not noticed how bad the weather was or how dangerous the conditions had become. In the days after the tragedies, the Sherpas, who know Everest better than anyone, told us they had never seen the mountain in such dangerous conditions.

It was the accidents and the resulting trauma that convinced us of the necessity to change our plan. We had no choice. Ten of our strongest people were no longer with us; four people had died and six of our leading climbers had left the team. The tragedies had shaken us out of our complacency, and we had been forced to develop our peripheral vision to see everything around us as we struggled to keep our dream alive.

A few years ago, while researching a book I commissioned called *One Step Beyond: Rediscovering the Adventure Attitude*, the author, Alan Hobson, asked me to describe the meaning of the word adventure. The answer has defined my life ever since. I replied: "Adventure isn't hanging on a rope on the side of Mount Everest. That is just one arena where we choose to pursue our goals. Adventure is an attitude that we must apply to daily life; facing new challenges, seizing new opportunities, testing our physical and mental resources against the unknown and, in the process, discovering our own unique potential."

It is this approach to life that is at the root of all One Step Beyond WorldWide programs (see Chapter Twelve). I believe that the use of adventure as a metaphor for life can create a new paradigm for us all as we struggle with rapid change. I am confident that the Adventure Attitude offers a light at the end of the tunnel as we contemplate the precarious transition into the next millennium of challenge.

In spring 1986, a second Canadian expedition went to Mount Everest to attempt to climb the west ridge from the north side of the mountain in Tibet. On that team were six members of our 1982 expedition, some of whom I had met departing from base camp after the tragedies. Also on that team was Sharon Wood, a twenty-nine-year-old mountain guide from my home town of Canmore, who was soon to become a key associate in the One Step Beyond WorldWide organization.

On May 20, 1986, after months of struggle and just as night was falling, Sharon and her climbing companion Dwayne Congdon reached the top of the world. At that point, Sharon became the first North American woman to achieve that amazing feat and only the sixth woman in history to climb Everest.

Sharon Wood does not look like the kind of individual who could climb the world's highest mountain. She is a slim, attractive woman, who is now the proud mother of two fine sons. When she speaks before audiences of business executives, many are moved to ask what it was that got her to the top. Sharon answers, "I discovered it wasn't a matter of physical strength, but a matter of psychological strength. The conquest lay within my own mind to penetrate those barriers of self-imposed limitations and get through to that good stuff, the stuff called potential, ninety percent of which we rarely use."

I believe that what Sharon is talking about is attitude. Clearly, attitude is the key to success. We can have all the education, all the knowledge, all the experience in the world, but if we carry the wrong attitude in our minds, we are doomed to failure. The academic world agrees! A recent study of successful people by the Carnegie Institute concluded that eighty-five percent of success was attributed solely to mental attitude.

Similarly, our perception of the challenges we face in life is often more significant than the reality of the challenges themselves. In the words of Laurie Skreslet, who was the first of our team to reach Everest's summit: "It's not what you go through in life that makes you what you are; it's how you react to the world you're going through."

It is this approach to life that forms the roots of the Adventure Attitude, a philosophy that enables forward-looking people to meet the challenges of change with optimism and to deal with uncertainty as an exciting adventure. It is an approach that can be summarized by using the acronym: ADVENTURE.

The Adventure Attitude offers nine keys to happiness, fulfillment and success in life, no matter in what arena you are operating or what adversity you are struggling to overcome.

Here are the nine keys of the Adventure Attitude:

A	—	Adaptability
D	—	Desire and Determination
V	—	Vision & Values
E	—	Experience
N	—	Natural Curiosity
T	—	Teamwork & Trust
U	—	Unlimited Optimism
R	—	Risk-ability
E	—	Exceptional Performance

When I look at these nine basic principles, it becomes evident that achieving success in life is really quite simple. But we live today in a very complex world where events on the opposite side of the earth, over which we have no direct control, are inexorably changing the way we live our lives. It is easy to become distracted and to lose focus.

In the final analysis, it is important to realize that the Adventure Attitude has been crucial to the evolution of society over the centuries. As the world has changed throughout history, so have the people who struggled through those times, but they moved ahead despite the uncertainty.

In these challenging times, so must we!

A — ADAPTABILITY

Change is not merely necessary to life.
It is life! By the same token, life is adaptation.
—*Alvin Toffler*

When Pat Morrow became the second member of our team to climb Everest, he achieved a goal that was only part of his ultimate dream: to become the first person in the world to stand on the summits of the highest mountain in each of the seven continents. Everest for Pat was just the highest mountain in Asia!

As one of the world's finest professional adventure photographers, Pat was consumed with the need to take a series of shots from this ultimate point on earth. But on the summit that day, the temperature was so cold that the battery charging his camera could not function. He could not get a reading of the light, which he knew would be essential to enable him to expose his film accurately. So in the subzero temperatures, he removed his insulating gloves and started to manually operate the exposure setting on the camera, taking multiple pictures of the same view, each one with a slightly different setting of the exposure meter.

On a single lens reflex camera, these settings are called f-stops, and there are numerous settings, all the way from f-1.4

to f-32. By using all the settings, Pat knew he could get one photograph of each view (and only one) that would be perfectly exposed to the light at the top of the world.

Because of this focus and concentration, Pat Morrow brought back some of the best photographs ever taken from Everest's summit. Many people have since asked him his secret. How does he take such magnificent photographs? His answer is intriguing! With considerable understatement, he says, "f-8 . . . and be there!" That's how you take great photographs—f-8 the camera, so it is correctly exposed to the light, and be there to click the shutter. It's that simple!

But I think there is a more important meaning behind his phrase!

The phrase "f-8 . . . and be there!" is all about adapting to change in daily life. It is the perfect metaphor of the need for constant adaptation in the increasingly complex society in which we all live today. Just as Pat Morrow must f-8 his camera to expose it correctly to the light at the top of Everest, so must we f-8 our minds to expose them correctly to the constant change in the world around us. We must also be there to meet the day-to-day challenges, because we can no longer do things today the way we might have operated in decades past. The world has changed, and we must change with it.

The phrase "f-8... and be there!" is a metaphor for continuous improvement and for the positive dissatisfaction that we must constantly maintain in our quest to become better at what we do.

Every day I ask myself the question: How can I f-8 my mind today better than it was yesterday? What has changed in my world today that wasn't here yesterday? How can I be there today better than I was yesterday? How can I more accurately expose my mind today to the reality of tomorrow's challenges? It is part of the ongoing battle I fight against complacency. And it is central to my struggle to achieve exceptional performance in everything I do.

Creativity evolves over time; through osmosis you glean ideas from those with whom you are working.

—*Pat Morrow*

D — DESIRE AND DETERMINATION

You've got to hang on to your dreams.
Great dreams don't happen overnight.

Dr. Layne Longfellow, with whom I taught the highly acclaimed Banff Wilderness Seminars during the six years I spent at the Banff Centre for Continuing Education, once commented that in his opinion there are two groups of students in high school: the insies and the outsies. The insies are the children who make it in school, the academic achievers, the kids who play on the football team or who are on the cheerleading squad. They are the students everyone wants to be associated with or everyone tries to emulate. On the other side are the outsies, those who try hard to make it, but consistently fall short. They are never quite able to attain their dreams.

I was definitely an outsie!

Layne goes on to say that in adult life, it is often the outsies who become more successful because they have struggled throughout their youth and carry forward these memories to adulthood, determined to prove to themselves and others that they are capable of high achievement in their lives.

When I look back today, I realize this is exactly what has motivated me throughout my adult years. It was the continuing desire to prove myself that took me up the Troll Wall, up Everest and on to form the One Step Beyond WorldWide corporation.

But it was also a determination rooted in the values and beliefs implanted in my mind by my parents and teachers during childhood. In particular, it is the belief that once you have started something, you should keep striving, learning and adapting no matter what setbacks you might experience along the way. It all started when my father said, "If you turn around now, you'll regret it for the rest of your life," during that cold, wet hike up Ben Nevis in Scotland when I was eleven.

In the aftermath of the second accident on the Everest climb, in which cameraman Blair Griffiths died and Dave Read was buried alive in the bowels of a crevasse, Dave's immediate reaction was to give up. That night, as the three survivors staggered into base camp, he declared that he would leave the expedition and go home where it was safe. But two days later, after he had divorced himself from the emotion of the incident and had time to reflect on the experience and learn its lessons, searching deeply within his soul for the internal resources to continue, he decided to return to the challenge.

He later told me that the single most important factor in his decision was the realization that his father would have expected him to keep going in the face of this adversity.

The lesson, I think, is clear. It is vital that we not give up on our dreams when setbacks occur along the journey through life. In fact, at the time of greatest difficulty, we must think back to the beginning and revisit the reasons we started along our particular path in the first place.

When we set goals for ourselves and contemplate taking the first steps, we should consider the risks inherent in the journey. If we find the risks acceptable, we must then commit to action and not give up when the going gets tough.

Our commitment to our goals in life is rooted in our values and beliefs. Thus, it becomes important that we understand these values and beliefs, and can clearly articulate them and learn to live by them as we face the constant challenges of modern life.

But, just as importantly, we must move beyond procrastination, accept the risks and begin the journey.

Whatever you can do, or dream you can, begin it.
Boldness has genius, power, and magic in it.
—Goethe

V — VISION & VALUES

Vision . . . is the ability to:
Look to the past and learn from it;
Look to the present and be attuned to it;
Look to the future and be prepared for it.
—Unknown

What really is vision? A sense of direction? An idea of where you want to go? An imaginary path through life? I don't think it is any one of these things, but all of them.

In its simplest form, vision is what this book is all about!

If I were asked to identify a vision for my own life, I would have to say it is to make a contribution, to leave the world a better place than when I entered it and to help others enhance their self-esteem and sense of fulfillment through climbing their own Everests in life, just as I have been able to climb mine.

Vision is what separates the great achievers from the also-rans. It is a distinguishing characteristic of great leaders.

In 1993, the Institute for the Future, a highly respected corporate forecasting organization, located in Menlo Park, California, predicted in their ten-year forecast that global leaders of the twenty-first century would be "visionary" and "adventurous." In particular, they predicted that successful leaders of the next millennium would build their success on the following personal characteristics:

- Patient but persistent
- Humble (as compared to modest)
- Willing to fail and learn from failures

- Possessing a good sense of humor (laughing with, not at, other perspectives)
- Strongly imaginative
- Emotionally stable
- Curious, socially and intellectually
- Perceptually acute, but willing to postpone judgments, sometimes indefinitely
- Capable of listening well
- Intuitive about communication (particularly nonverbal) across cultures
- Comfortable with discomfort
- Comfortable with uncertainty

I find the need to be "perceptually acute, but willing to postpone judgments, sometimes indefinitely" to be of particular significance.

Clearly, the pace of change in the next century will be so great that we will not have the luxury of coming to firm conclusions about what is happening in our lives. We will need to have an intuitive sense of what is occurring, but must remain flexible in adjusting to the constant changes that will be taking place around us. If we ever reach a definite judgment, we will have been left behind, because the factors that led to that conclusion will already have changed.

Interestingly enough, these characteristics also define the traditional adventurer, someone who is willing to dream great dreams, to endure through adversity, to take carefully considered risks and learn lessons from setbacks and is willing to embrace different cultures with an open mind. Adventurers are people who seek out the excitement of increasing uncertainty and who have the vision to seek out the opportunities that change can create.

It follows that we must all become great adventurers if we are to succeed in the complex world of the twenty-first century.

How we choose to perceive our circumstances is one of the most important choices we will ever make. People are not always born equal in terms of ability, but we have an equal opportunity in our choice of attitude. In the final analysis, our achievements, our failures, and how we face the challenges we are presented with is mostly a matter of perspective.

—*Carl Hiebert*

E — EXPERIENCE

The only failure in life is when we fail to learn the lessons from our experience.

My friend and mentor Layne Longfellow once suggested to me, "Experience that is unconsidered remains experience, but experience that is considered and digested becomes learning."

Clearly, we all have many experiences in our lives, some good, some bad. In fact, life is one long process of accumulating experiences one after another. In the busy lives we live today, some of us seem to be rushing from one experience to another, not taking time out to think about what is going on; in effect, becoming experience junkies.

But experience for the sake of experience is not enough. What types of experiences should we be seeking? Easy, comfortable ones? Or challenging experiences that will stretch our potential?

In my own life, I can honestly say that the most vivid experiences, and the ones from which I learned the biggest lessons, were those in which I was stretched to the limit, both physically and mentally. As the German philosopher Friedrich Nietzsche once wrote, "The secret of knowing the most fertile experiences and greatest joys in life is to live dangerously." As Sharon Wood has stated, the importance of struggle is that it forces us "to penetrate the self-imposed limitations in our minds" so we can discover the real potential within, "ninety percent of which we rarely use."

I believe that to achieve complete fulfillment in our lives we must consciously seek out new experiences; not be content with the comfortable existence we have created in the past, but constantly seek out new challenges and move forward into the unknown. It is the quest for new experience and new knowledge that has defined human progress throughout the centuries, and it is the same quest that will carry us forward into the new millennium.

So what is it that limits our ability to move ahead? What is it that creates the panic in our minds when we move from the known world of the past to the uncertain world of future opportunity? Partly, it is ego—the fear of being made to look a fool in front of our peers. But mostly, I think, it's the fear of failure.

But what is failure? If we try something we've never done before and don't quite attain the results we anticipated, is this a failure? If we learn something from our experience, can we in fact be said to have failed?

Personally, I don't think so! If we come out of a negative experience with more knowledge than when we started, we've not failed. We may have experienced a setback, but we're stronger because of the learning that took place. In fact, I think the only true failure in life is when we fail to learn the lessons from our experiences. If we try something twice and achieve the same negative results, then we haven't learned the first time around and we've truly failed.

There is no doubt in my mind that I am the person I am today because of all the experiences I have accumulated in my life, both good and bad. I can honestly state that I have learned something from every situation, even when it seemed at the time that I had failed. There is a lesson to be learned in everything we do, but we must set our minds to seek out the learning and to not let these opportunities pass us by.

When the accidents on Everest occurred early in the climb, it would have been very easy to have abandoned the expedition. In fact, my initial reaction was to do just that! How long, I asked myself, could we keep going when people were dying? When would enough be enough? Then I realized that we had not caused the tragedies. The accidents were not due to our negligence. We had just been in the wrong place at the wrong time. It was impossible to predict exactly when an avalanche might fall or where ice might collapse. We could not change the facts by giving up, but we could learn vital lessons from the situation. It was that acceptance, and the resultant change of plans, that eventually made it possible for us to go all the way to the top.

Today, whenever some difficulty strikes and I find myself in an uncomfortable situation, I think of those tough days on Everest and say to myself: This is happening. I cannot change the fact that it is happening. So what can I learn from the experience? By using this approach, I come out of every situation stronger than I went in.

The challenge of change in today's world demands that we seek out new experiences. There is no choice. Change is inevitable. We cannot change the fact that change is occurring. So we should always ask ourselves: What we can learn from the struggle?

When it's serious, that's when you make the biggest advances in your life. That's when you learn the important lessons.
—Laurie Skreslet

N — NATURAL CURIOSITY

If we're not pushing our limits, we're not discovering anything new.

Human beings are inherently curious.

Think of the children in your life today. Think of yourself when you were a child. Children are out there every day, pushing their limits, discovering their strengths and limitations, seeking more knowledge about the world in which they live. Children do not search for comfort and security. In fact, they reject the comfort of the known world in their constant quest for the unknown.

But as adults, we often find ourselves in a different arena. We start careers, take out mortgages, enter into relationships and start families. In effect, we move into a life-style where we have responsibilities. As adults, it is harder to maintain the curiosity we innately displayed when we were kids.

Without curiosity, however, we don't continue to grow. It is curiosity that drives us to seek out new opportunities and allows us to enter into new arenas of challenge. It is curiosity that has driven all great progress throughout history.

Why did Alexander Graham Bell invent the telephone? Because he was curious to see if communication over vast distances could be achieved.

Why do people bungee-jump from high bridges? Because they are curious to experience the rush of adrenaline and to feel that sense of complete commitment when they leap forward into the void. Truly, once you are on the way down, there is no way back!

Why did I want to climb the Troll Wall when everybody told me it was impossible? Because I was curious to see what it was like up there with five thousand feet of space below my heels. I needed to discover if I was up to the challenge and see what I could learn from the experience.

Without curiosity, there would be no future opportunities to which we might look forward.

So how do we strive to cultivate our curiosity?

By rejecting complacency. By continually seeking out new opportunities. By trying new things, even if we're not certain of the outcomes. Unless we try something new, we will never discover what we might become.

Although it becomes increasingly difficult as we grow older, we should never allow ourselves to be completely satisfied with our achievements in life. Once we become satisfied, complacency will set in and we will start to repeat things we have done before.

We must learn to apply positive dissatisfaction, being constantly dissatisfied with our performance or knowledge, but in a positive way to foster learning. It is this process of continuous improvement that separates the winners from the losers. It is curiosity that motivates us to expand our horizons and that defines who will achieve the greatest satisfaction in life.

In many ways, I think of myself today as a reincarnated explorer from the past. I have always been fascinated by stories of great explorers, people who were in the right place at the right time to make important geographic discoveries: Columbus, Champlain, Mackenzie and Peary, first to reach the North Pole. Those were the great days of adventure.

Today, there are few geographic unknowns on earth, but there is unlimited opportunity to explore other arenas. In fact, I am an explorer in my world just as Columbus was in his. It's just that I live in a different world. I'm exploring myself and the world in which I live, and I'm never going to be satisfied until I know everything about this world. In other words, I intend to explore until I die. I will always be discovering I intend my life to be an upward trajectory from birth to death, from the bottom to the top.

This is the mountain that we set out to climb at birth. As George Leigh Mallory wrote in 1924: "This is the struggle of life itself, *upwards and forever upwards*." It will be interesting to see what it will be like at the top. Who knows what we might learn along the way!

Reaching the summit is not the significant thing, because you learn nothing on the top. It's during the journey to the top that the learning takes place. The important thing is to digest the experience—to learn what it was that got you there. Then you can apply this new knowledge to the future.

T — TEAMWORK AND TRUST

Rarely do we achieve complete success in today's changing world without the help and support of others. The essence of teamwork is to identify and use the strengths of others to offset our own limitations, so that the strength of the team becomes greater than the sum of the individual parts.

If there is one principle in the Adventure Attitude that is best defined by the Everest experience, it is teamwork. Simply stated, it is teamwork that puts you on top.

Imagine a jigsaw puzzle, where every member of the team has a piece of the puzzle. If one person fails to put his or her piece of that puzzle into place, then the picture can never be complete and the goal of climbing to the top can never be achieved.

Nobody can achieve complete success in life without the help and support of others. As individuals, we all have strengths and limitations. It is these that make us unique. We have to build upon our strengths and try to improve upon our limitations.

In effective teamwork, we use the strengths of others to offset our limitations; synergistically, the strength of the team becomes greater than the strength of the individuals on the team.

In organizations, we also see strengths and limitations. We need to be very frank about identifying these. What do we do best, given our strengths and limitations? We should choose our goals accordingly.

And let us not forget to recognize the contributions of individual members of the team. Our egos seem to demand recognition. If we don't get it, we will not be members of the team for very long.

In the lead up to the Everest climb, I was well aware that my chances of reaching the summit were slim. There were other team members better prepared than I to do that particular job. But as the key organizer, I also had a critical role to play. If I could do my job to the best of my ability, then I knew we could put ourselves in a position where the summit climbers could do theirs. Having set my expectations accordingly, I was completely fulfilled when Laurie and Pat reached the summit, because when one person reaches the summit of Everest, the entire team climbs the mountain. And, having climbed Everest in my own terms, I would never go back. I believe that in life we must constantly be moving ahead, going one step beyond our previous experience.

Back in the spring of 1953, when Everest was still unclimbed, a British team set out to try to become the first to reach the top of the world. By mid-May, they were poised to push for the peak. Building on the supreme efforts of all the climbers on the expedition, two men finally reached the south peak of the mountain, more than 28,750 feet above the sea. They were the first to reach the foot of the final ridge, just 250 feet away from the highest point on earth.

It was mid-afternoon and the two looked toward the summit that glittered above them; it must have seemed so close, they could reach out and touch it. They were strongly attracted by the glory that could be theirs if they went all the way. They would be world-famous. Their names would be on the front page of every newspaper, and nobody could ever again be first.

But it was getting late in the day and they were concerned that if they went on, they could get into trouble. They had already climbed far above their camp and were worried about what might happen if darkness trapped them. Would they have to be rescued? Would the entire carefully planned and implemented team effort collapse because of their selfish ambition in wanting to go to the peak? But they were so close!

Struggling to make the right decision, they argued and debated about what to do. Their ambition told them to go on, but their responsibility to the team dictated that they should go down.

Finally, reluctantly, they decided to turn their backs on the glory of the peak and retreat to the security of their tents, some three thousand feet below.

In my presentations, I sometimes suggest that their decision to turn back is analogous to Neil Armstrong descending from the lunar module to the last rung of the ladder in 1969—and then not making that giant leap for mankind onto the surface of the moon!

As the two climbers descended from their high point, they carefully avoided the ladder of steps they had kicked in the snow that morning, and they left ropes in all the difficult and dangerous places.

Three days later, after the assault camp had been moved to 27,900 feet, Edmund Hillary and Tenzing Norgay climbed up those steps and pulled up on those ropes. With the extra strength and time at their disposal, they crossed the final ridge and climbed onto the highest peak on earth, 29,028 feet above sea level. In doing so, they became the men we know today as the conquerors of Mount Everest.

I think the lesson from this story is clear. Although Hillary and Norgay were the first to reach the summit, it was a British *team* that climbed the mountain. And while Hillary and Norgay deserved their fame and success, they were really just the lucky ones who were in the right place at the right time.

In my opinion, the real heroes of that 1953 ascent were not Hillary and Norgay, but the two climbers who have been long since forgotten: Tom Bourdillon and Charles Evans. They were the men who turned their backs on personal glory only 250 feet from the peak in order to maximize and even guarantee success for the team two days later.

When you see one person standing on top of Everest, or attaining any major goal in life, it is important to recognize the contribution of all the people who put him or her there.

I don't think the only heroes of our success on Everest were the climbers and the Sherpas on the mountain. The heroes included the families who stayed home to maintain the stable base: the moms and dads, wives, girlfriends and kids; they were the ones who allowed their sons, husbands, boyfriends and fathers to go and take this chance on Everest, so far away. They took the *real* risk, knowing that if we didn't do this thing, we could never be the people we wanted to be, nor could we be the people they wanted us to be.

We learned much from the experience—and I think our loved ones did, too. We all became better people for the struggle that we endured during those difficult days on the top of the world.

When you come to a wall, either you climb over it or you go back. But once you've given up, you can't go back and redo it. You only go around once.

—John Hughes

U — UNLIMITED OPTIMISM

Life is a leap of faith. There is no way that we can know what will happen tomorrow.

Have you ever seen a successful pessimist? I doubt it! Pessimism is negative, and pessimistic people exude negative energy. They look for the worst in each situation and usually find it. Our minds have this wonderful ability to create the results we project and desire, particularly if we work at it hard enough. Pessimists will always take the low road and, while they may achieve some success in their lives, will always have the feeling that they have not quite made it.

If our minds can help us create the results we desire, why not take the high road and remain optimistic in every situation? Sure, let's be realistic about our problems, but let's always look for the good that can come from every experience.

In just about every adventure in which I have been involved, we were forced to regroup before final success was achieved. On the Troll Wall and Sondre Trolltind in Norway, bad weather dictated a retreat after our first tentative forays into the unknown. On Everest, we were struck by tragedies after such a positive beginning to the climb. When pioneering a new route to the top of previously unclimbed mountains in the Canadian Arctic, I have often been forced back before finding the weaknesses in the mountain's defenses that would lead to the summit.

In such situations, it would have been easy to have folded my tent and gone home. But my desire to create the future and to attain my goal always wins out. I always know that an open mind and an optimistic attitude, given time and patience, will lead to the top.

We hear a lot these days about how our living standards are deteriorating from what we have been led to believe is our birthright in modern society. For the first time, we are told that our children may have a lower standard of living than we have. My reaction is: So what? Who said things had to continue to improve forever? Why shouldn't our children learn the value of struggle the way we or our predecessors did? Only by investing in our own future, by learning the value of effort and struggling to climb our own mountains, can we really come to appreciate what we have in life.

That is one of the great things about climbing—when you voluntarily put yourself out on a limb and take the risk, you appreciate all the more what you have in the valley when you come down.

I am an eternal optimist in everything I do; I'm not merely content to sit back and let things happen. I use all my resources to learn from my experiences and create new opportunities for myself. I have learned long ago that human beings will not change until forced to change, until our attention is riveted on the problems we face. In this context, we can only be optimistic about the future.

We have the ability to fix all our problems. We have the ingenuity and the intellectual power to find adaptive solutions to every situation. But we must use our minds to think and to question, and not complacently continue to operate by habit, doing things the way we have always done them.

Our young people are unlike those of previous generations. They have different skills and different experiences. They are better equipped than their parents to handle the world of the twenty-first century. They will have just as many opportunities in their lives as we have had in ours. We should encourage them with optimism and not dampen their attitudes with negative thoughts.

In the final analysis, life is a leap of faith. There is no way we can predict exactly what will happen to us tomorrow, next week or next year. We can make some intelligent guesses, but nobody can know for sure. This is the adventure of life. It is exciting to be surprised. Let's enjoy the challenge with unlimited optimism and take the high road to success.

You either change, or you stagnate.
You either leap forward, or you fall backward.
You cannot stay where you are today!

R — RISK-ABILITY

The only limiting factor to our achievements
in life is our fear of the unknown.

If adaptability is the ability to adapt, then risk-ability is the ability to take risks. We all have that ability, because life is a risk. Believe it or not, we all take risks every day without really thinking about them. When we get out of bed in the morning, we initiate a process of risk-taking that only concludes when we go back to bed at night. But most of these risks are so much a part of our lives that we don't even acknowledge them.

My friend and climbing companion Rusty Baillie, with whom I shared the risk on Sondre Trolltind and Everest, once gave me this poem.

To laugh is to risk appearing the fool.
To weep is to risk appearing sentimental.
To reach out for another is to risk involvement.
To expose feelings is to risk exposing our true selves.
To place your ideas, your dreams before the crowd is to risk loss.
To love is to risk not being loved in return.
To live is to risk dying.
To hope is to risk despair.
To try is to risk failure.
But risk we must, for the greatest hazard in life is to risk nothing.
The man, the woman, who risks nothing does nothing,
    has nothing, is nothing.

Inexorably linked to risk, of course, is fear. Every time we move forward in life, we are forced to leave something behind. When we leave something behind, we take a risk. When we take a risk, we feel fear. It is a natural human reaction to the unknown. So when we feel fear, we must find the courage to overcome it, otherwise we will not progress. The great American writer Mark Twain defined courage as "resistance to fear, mastery of fear—not the absence of fear." In its simplest form, courage is the ability to get up in the morning and confront daily life.

One of the things I learned early on climbing the Troll Wall was that when you run away from fear, it grows in your mind, but when you move toward fear and attack it directly, it recedes. The hardest part of that climb was simply getting started. The night before, I had lain awake consumed by fear, tormented by all the things that might go wrong up on that unknown precipice, wondering why I was putting myself into such a precarious situation and fighting the temptation to turn around and go home. But I knew that unless I started to climb the next day, I would never discover if I was up to the challenge.

My climbing companion, Tony Howard, accurately captured the mood of that moment in a subsequent article:

> Once admitted, fear gnaws away at your subconscious; it prods and probes at every chink in your mental armour. It can mushroom into a nightmare of emotion from which there is no release until dawn; the slow dawn that lights the sky with a golden glow, yet refuses to burst over the black horizon. You wish to hell the sun would hurry. The dark, gloomy rock leers down from above you, hostile, overwhelming, unknown.
>
> Finally, you can stand it no longer, the silence, the restless night-long shuffle of your comrades, the dark unfriendly rock, above all, the inactivity; just waiting, eternally waiting and thinking, second after second ticking slowly, inexorably into minutes, into long, long hours. The thoughts multiply, obsess you and devour you. You wish you had never set foot on rock; you decide the whole venture is too big for you, and you can only sit and wait, a victim of your own weakness.

How many of us can remember sleepless nights worrying about a problem we must face the following day? How many entrepreneurs have stayed awake, wondering where they will find the next dollar? How many have suffered through the long night hours, consumed by fears of what might be? And how many of us can remember getting up in the morning, confronting the issue and discovering that the reality was not as bad as our imagination had conjured?

When forced to confront fear, a lot of people step back. But those who step forward will move forward. All of us have great dreams in life, but our potential to achieve these dreams is constrained by fear of the unknown. If we can find the courage to overcome fear, if we can move toward fear and take the first step, we might just succeed. But we'll never know until we start!

It's how I deal with challenge that makes the critical difference —I can let it control me, or I can control it.

—*Sharon Wood*

E — EXCEPTIONAL PERFORMANCE

Achievement is the constant process of going one step beyond your previous experience.

Exceptional performance is at the root of all high achievement in life and is evident in successful people by their constant desire to go one step beyond in everything they do. It is a philosophy that completely rejects complacency and that demands the inexorable exploration of human potential. It is this constant exploration of possibility that defines my belief that better is always possible.

Equally important is the quest for lifelong learning. Eric Hoffer once noted: "In times of change, learners inherit the earth, while the learned find themselves beautifully equipped to deal with a world that no longer exists."

We must all view life as a great adventure, as an opportunity to be seized.

The world we live in today is a world that was developed through the spirit of adventure of the pioneers who settled the land. They were people who left behind the security of the known to test themselves against the unknown. In doing so, they committed to action and took risks, recognizing they would be asked to take personal responsibility for the consequences of their decisions.

Nowadays we live in such comfortable urban settings that we have lost track of that spirit. Governments provide every kind of security imaginable and there is a tendency to no longer be personally accountable. Security is, of course, the very worst thing we can create, because once we have built a secure world, we cease to challenge ourselves and to evolve as a positive society.

The challenge of change forces us to rethink our values and rekindle our spirit of adventure. It takes courage, resourcefulness and endurance to meet challenge: courage to try, to commit and to take risks; resourcefulness to be innovative and creative in finding new ways to do old things; endurance to keep going when the going gets tough.

Change represents a great opportunity, and we must welcome it with optimism. We will be forced to live on the edge in a way that all human beings were meant to live.

Attitude is the key to success—not skill, not knowledge, not education—ATTITUDE!

ELEVEN

LIVING WITH THE ADVENTURE ATTITUDE

Courage is resistance to fear, mastery of fear—not the absence of fear.
—Mark Twain

IN MY FIRST BOOK, *ONE Step Beyond: Rediscovering the Adventure Attitude*, in which I collaborated with writer Alan Hobson, we profiled Laurie Skreslet, John Hughes, Mike Beedell, Sharon Wood and Laurie Dexter to investigate the underlying philosophy that drove them to climb Mount Everest, to sail around the world single-handed or to ski across the frozen Arctic Ocean via the North Pole. In the process of interviewing these five high achievers, we discovered that more important than their actual achievements was what they learned from their experiences and how they applied this new knowledge to other challenges in their lives.

What evolved was a simple recipe for success that can be followed by all people who want to make the most of themselves and the world in which they live—a formula for meeting the challenges of changing times. This is the Adventure Attitude.

So the question now becomes: How? How do *we* apply the Adventure Attitude in our daily lives? How do *we* change the way we operate in a changing world?

Here are the basic steps:

Step 1: *Get in touch with your core values and basic beliefs. Understand what is really important to you. Don't concern yourself with security, material wealth, fame, fortune, power of position. Do concern yourself with contentment, satisfaction, freedom, independence and happiness.*

One of the notable things about people with the Adventure Attitude is that they don't subscribe to traditional definitions of success: a big house, two cars, membership in the country club. To them, success in life is only to be found in achieving a high measure of self-satisfaction and contentment. They know what they want out of life and are prepared to take leadership in setting their own course; they are not concerned with the expectations of others, but with acting in accordance with their own clearly defined core values and basic beliefs. It follows that you must know what is important to you, and you must be able to clearly articulate your own personal values and beliefs.

Step 2: *Dare to dream. Dream BIG! Then decide on your ultimate goals. Carefully evaluate the risks in moving ahead. If you find them to be acceptable, take the first step. Then commit to the effort with everything you have.*

It is important to dream and to dream big, but dreaming is not enough. You must take the first step toward achieving those dreams. Because if you don't take that first committed step, then nothing else can happen. Thousands, if not millions, of great dreams never see the light of day because the people who dream them are too fearful to leave behind the comforts of their present lives and move into the future. If you want to make something happen in your life, begin the journey, keep your eye firmly focused on the goal and never give up on the dream. You may not get to that goal as easily as you had hoped, but as long as you know where you want to go, you will eventually get there.

Step 3: *Find the courage to overcome your natural fear of the unknown. Step out from the crowd and soak in the excitement of increasing uncertainty. Cultivate your curiosity and maintain positive dissatisfaction with the way things are. Actively seek out the unpredictable; digest your experience and convert it to your own positive advantage.*

It's natural that you should feel some element of fear when you try something you've never tried before. This is nature's way of focusing your mind on a problem. If you recognize what's happening within your mind, you can push the fear aside and move ahead. It's exciting to face the unknown! It's the way life was meant to be lived. Imagine how boring everything would be if you could predict exactly what was going to happen today, tomorrow, next year. Stay dissatisfied, but in a positive way, seeking out new challenges, searching for new learning opportunities and continually striving to discover what the future can offer.

Step 4: *Ignore the doubting Thomases and endure adversity by remaining focused on your goal. Never, never, never give up!*

When you leave the beaten path and start doing new and innovative things, you will become a threat to others around you who are complacently continuing to do things the way they have always done them. Their negativism can become a challenge. But if you can maintain your focus and ignore what they are saying, you can use their negative energy as a catalyst to prove them wrong and attain your objective. When someone tells you that you cannot do something because it does not agree with the norm or maintain the status quo, you must become even more determined to find a way to succeed. In doing so, you will derive great pride from being different and draw considerable satisfaction from being a leader, going where nobody has gone before.

Step 5: *Forget failure. Erase the word from your vocabulary and learn the lessons from your setbacks. Always ask yourself what you can learn from the struggle.*

If you don't try something new in life, you will never know what you are capable of achieving. When you try something new, there is always the possibility that you won't quite attain the goal you expect. But this is not failure! You have learned a lesson and you have more knowledge as a result. To grow in your life and to discover more of the potential that lies within, you must accept the setbacks along the way. But it is absolutely essential that you reflect on the outcome of each setback, think about what has happened to you and learn the lessons. Then you can apply this new information to the journey that lies ahead and establish new challenges that will stretch you in their attainment.

Step 6: *Accept the inevitability of change in a changing world. Adapt creatively to new situations by finding new ways of doing old things. Trust your intuition to be your guide.*

A little reflection will tell you that change is the only real constant you can expect in life. The world you live in today is different from that of your progenitors. You are a different person because you have experienced things that would have been inconceivable in their lives. Given that change is inevitable, you can accept change as either a positive or negative force. You can use change to your advantage or let it consume you with worries and fear. What does your intuition say in this situation? Act on that intuition, because your gut reaction is usually the best decision-making tool in your arsenal. Once you have made the intuitive step forward, you will find the path ahead much more clearly defined because you will have left behind the confusing cloak of procrastination and will have gained access to all of your resources to prove to yourself (and others) that you are on the right path.

Step 7: Remain passionately optimistic, enthusiastic and positive. Turn obstacles into opportunities, failures into successes, disappointments into direction. Remember that success is a journey, not a destination.

This is where your attitude becomes crucial. You must choose whether to take the high road to success or the low road to failure. Keep your eye on the goal and stay confident, positive and optimistic in every situation you face. Continually check your feelings and evaluate the way you react to every situation. It is very easy to slip into negativism when things go wrong. Keep your eye fixed firmly on the horizon and don't worry about the little things that may not occur exactly as you hoped.

Step 8: Work productively within a team, trust others and value their contribution, but always be personally accountable for the consequences of your own actions.

To achieve your greatest ambitions, you must become a team player, not consumed solely with your own ego and ambition, but seeking greater impact through the synergy a team working toward a common goal engenders. Within that framework, you must always take complete personal responsibility for yourself and not blame others when something goes wrong. If you have embarked upon a course of action and have fully considered the consequences of your decision, there is nobody but you to look to when you face the setbacks along the way.

Step 9: When you've given it your all, soak in the satisfaction of ultimate achievement. Success breeds self-confidence, self-esteem and self-worth.

If it has been a struggle and you have come out on top, you will have grown immeasurably through the experience. Although it may not have been easy, you can reflect upon your success and build the confidence that leads to better things. The tougher the struggle, the more you can enjoy the achievement because you now know that you only really appreciate those things in life that you have been forced to work hard to achieve. This is why the goals you now set must be difficult ones so you can continue to build your self-worth and self-esteem as you strive toward the next horizon of ambition.

Step 10: *Enjoy the moment, reflect on your journey, but reject complacency. It's time to move on to new challenges. To progress in life, you must constantly be climbing new mountains and seeking out new adventures.*

Reaching the summit is not the end of the climb, but the beginning of the next challenge. Success in one goal must be followed by the creation of new challenges. Otherwise, you will become complacent, living on past accomplishments and missing out on the opportunities that only now seem possible because of the learning that has taken place. It's time to move on to new challenges. Set new goals, new mountains to be climbed, and seek out the new adventures that are only to be found when you go where you haven't been before.

It's that simple! All you've got to do is *do* it—every minute, every hour, every day, throughout your entire life. Only then will you be able to say that you know what you are capable of achieving, because you will have discovered yourself.

Just Do It!
—*Nike advertisement*

TWELVE

JOURNEY TOWARD THE
NEXT MILLENNIUM

We are shaping the world faster than we can change ourselves and we are applying to the present the habits of the past.
—*Winston Churchill*

AS WE EMBARK UPON our journey toward the next millennium and contemplate the psychological shift from the known world of the twentieth century to the unknown world of the twenty-first, it becomes more and more clear that the attitudes and skills that brought success in the past will no longer be relevant for the future. Indeed, the next decade will represent one of the great transitional periods in world history. More than ever before, economic, political and social change will occur with lightning speed. It follows that we must start to prepare now for the exciting challenges ahead.

The One Step Beyond WorldWide organization is equipped to help you make that transition. Founded in 1983 out of my desire to go one step beyond Everest and to apply the lessons of Everest to corporate and professional life, the company has since grown into an international educational and motivational organization dedicated to meeting the challenges of change in modern society. Working with clients from across the globe, we have developed an enviable reputation based upon our unique use of the metaphor of adventure as a vehicle for helping individuals and organizations create the new attitudes and strategies needed for survival and success in the twenty-first century.

One Step Beyond WorldWide associates and global representatives are located in Canada, the United States, Puerto Rico and Latin America, Japan, Hong Kong, the Philippines, Malaysia, Singapore, Indonesia, Thailand, Australia, New Zealand, South Africa, the United Kingdom and the European community.

At One Step Beyond WorldWide, our vision is a world of global understanding, where each individual is adaptable in the face of uncertainty and where every action is considered with regard to its impact on the greater whole.

To play a meaningful role in the achievement of this vision, we have adopted a mission of encouraging individuals within organizations to increase the effectiveness of their contributions to themselves and others. Through the design and delivery of innovative educational experiences and by supporting the implementation of learning, we will assist people throughout the world to seek opportunities to go one step beyond.

In striving to achieve these objectives, we are committed to acting in accordance with our core values of ethical action, continuous learning and exceptional performance:

Ethical Action: We act with integrity. We operate on a basis of trust and a belief in ourselves and our clients. We treat each other with dignity and respect. We hold ourselves accountable for making a contribution to the greater common good.

Continuous Learning: We believe that curiosity, fun and adventure are at the root of learning. We encourage and support

John Amatt speaking before an audience of six thousand at the Million Dollar Round Table meeting held at Radio City Music Hall in New York.

continuous personal and organizational growth to assist ourselves and others to strive for full potential.

Exceptional Performance: We fully and consistently meet the needs of our clients and continually strive to go one step beyond their expectations and our own high standards.

The educational and motivational programs we deliver around the world are based on the philosophy articulated in my inspirational keynote presentation, *Climbing Your Own Everest: What It Takes To Get To The Top*, which explores the metaphor of striving to reach for the top of the world. Illustrated by magnificent color photography from the Everest climb and supplemented by music, sound effects and taped radio conversations, this presentation investigates the human qualities we must all bring to bear in climbing to the top in the difficult economic environments of today. Concepts that I explore include teamwork, commitment, setting realistic goals, adapting to changing conditions, and the role of a positive attitude, all set against our real life-and-death struggle on the mountain.

To enhance this presentation and to challenge corporations and professional groups to embrace change, take prudent risks, stretch beyond comfortable personal limits, meet commitments, and build teamwork and trust, we have also produced a series of multi-image videos based on the theme *Everest, The Ultimate Summit*. Available for rent in seven parts, these award-winning programs are designed to provide a thematic framework for business meetings that can benefit from the dramatic presentation of contemporary ideas using the metaphor and paradigm of adventure.

My more comprehensive, half-day corporate development workshops, called *Meeting the Challenge of Change*, focuses on the enhancement of organizational culture and philosophy, and builds upon much of the experience and approach outlined in this book. Individual components of this workshop investigate the following topics: The Mountain of Change; The Age of Discovery; Seven Keys to Meeting the Challenge (curiosity, courage, commitment, creativity, cooperation, communication and concentration); What It Takes To Get To The Top; Living with the Adventure Attitude; and Global Leaders of the Twenty-first Century.

In 1991, One Step Beyond WorldWide formed a strategic alliance with the Pacific Centre for Leadership to enhance our ability to design and deliver *Teampower!* seminars and *In Practice!* implementation consulting services. Corporate clients who enrol in these one- to five-day outdoor programs take part in experiential, problem-solving activities that develop the ability of participants to make creative, high-quality

Teampower! seminar participants tackle a simulated stretcher-lowering exercise in the Canadian Rockies.

decisions, take calculated risks, act with mutual trust and respect, communicate more effectively together, improve feedback skills and become accountable for the consequences of their own actions. The *In Practice!* consultations ensure that all learning is transferred back to the workplace.

Clients who have utilized these programs tell us they value our services because we focus on their business interests, translate our work directly into on-the-job applications and build and maintain highly supportive client relationships. In addition, they appreciate our willingness to innovate, adjusting our services to suit specific needs. And, most importantly, they value our dedication to results.

Over the years, *Teampower!* seminars have taken place at mountain resorts throughout North America, during sailing expeditions in the Caribbean and while rafting down white-water rivers.

With the year 2000 fast approaching, One Step Beyond WorldWide has embarked upon an ambitious global initiative for visionary twenty-first century corporations that will focus on the development of new attitudes, approaches and strategies within modern society as we enter into the unpredictable world of the next millennium. Known as *Global Odyssey 2000*, this initiative will bring together the resources of a select group of major sponsors to undertake a high-profile circumnavigation of the earth aboard a custom-designed tall ship. Using ship-to-shore satellite communications, this sailing odyssey will have three major goals:

- to research the philosophies of achievement in global cultures;
- to produce a television series and mass-market educational and motivational products for global distribution based upon recorded interviews with high achievers from all walks of life and in all societies visited; and
- to broadcast weekly live television programs via satellite that will allow schools throughout the world to integrate the Adventure Attitude into classroom discussions as the around-the-world odyssey unfolds.

In addition, we plan to sail into fifty major coastal cities, representing more than 130 million people in forty countries worldwide, and to stage high-impact, Straight to the Top . . . and Beyond educational events, designed to motivate global citizens from all walks of life to grasp the amazing opportunities offered by the coming century and to move forward into the new millennium with unlimited optimism and a mind free of self-imposed limitations.

Participation in this sailing odyssey will involve a journey of discovery, not only toward the next millennium, but *into* the increasingly globalised societies of the twenty-first century.

As I write today, I am embarking upon that journey. I intend to continue to explore my own new worlds for the rest of my life. It will be an exciting and stimulating quest.

Why not join me? If you are interested in our educational programs, or wish to learn more about the *Global Odyssey 2000* initiative, I invite you to write or call today:

John Amatt
President & CEO
One Step Beyond WorldWide
PO Box 990, Canmore, Alberta, Canada T0L 0M0
Phone: (403) 678-5255 / Fax: (403) 678-4534

Appendix A

How One Step Beyond WorldWide Clients
View the Relevance of the Adventure Attitude
in their Professional and Corporate Lives

On Team Spirit:

The feedback I received from our invited corporate clients, as well as from our own management staff, was exceptional. Having attended the seminar myself, I can indeed attest to the profound impact made on us by your vivid recollections and extraordinary slide presentation.

When we originally discussed the idea of your addressing the group, I admit to not fully comprehending how we could apply your experiences endured in such extreme conditions to our own everyday lives. It is now clear that all work environments rely on that same team spirit to reach common goals, and I am truly grateful to you for imparting such learned wisdom in such a human and touching manner.

Thomas Axmacher, General Manager
The Regent Hotel, Hong Kong

On the Climb to the Top:

John's presentation at both our Asian and European summits was spellbinding. His Everest story of teamwork, hardship and adversity was unique and captivated the entire audience. I believe everyone related to his story and felt as if they were with him and his Everest team as they climbed to the top of the world.

The analogy of climbing our own Everests with our daily hardships was brought to the forefront for everyone in the audience. Afterward, the attendees fully understood the pitfalls and barriers they would be facing on a daily measure. They also came to the realization that they could overcome their adversities in the same manner that John's team had overcome theirs.

It goes without saying that this was the most incredible presentation we have ever heard. The message was clear and all participants left with a feeling that they had climbed Everest that day. But more importantly, they now have a full understanding of what skills they need to climb their very own mountains. [The phrase] *f-8 . . . and be there* will forever be in our minds.

Joe Padgett, Director
International Marketing
Motorola Paging Products Group

On Risk and Adaptability:

Your talk was very inspiring and your messages were totally aligned to those we are delivering to our sales teams this year. You helped us focus on the importance of risk-taking, adaptability and teamwork, and you motivated all of us to rediscover our own adventure attitude.

Carly Fiorina, Sales Vice President
AT&T Network Systems

On Vision:

You have left us with a clear vision of what will be required of our managers, present and future: commitment, resourcefulness, endurance, flexibility to meet the challenge of change, and above all, the courage to keep a clear perspective of the goals in spite of any adversities.

> Bruce Aubin, Senior Vice-President
> Air Canada

On Taking the First Steps:

As a keynote speaker at our marketing conference held in Macau, John Amatt set the tone for delegates in aiming for the top, overcoming problems, anticipating needs and the essentials of teamwork.

His colorful and personal presentation carried the message of the importance of taking the first steps, the rewards of personal achievement, the necessity of cooperation and the survival issues of detailed planning for a successful outcome.

John's Everest experiences provided an excellent vehicle for focusing management and individual attitudes in a stimulating and memorable presentation.

> Sarah Benecke, Chief Executive Officer
> The Asian Sources Media Group

On Learning from our Experiences:

This is my second day back in the office and before any more time passes I want to say thank you for the outstanding contribution you made to the success of our meeting held in Hawaii last week. I had great expectations of your presentation, both as to its content and the impact that it would have on our people—and my expectations were surpassed! I heard many conversations during the balance of the week that reflected upon what you had to say and its application to the difficult task ahead of us the next five years. I am sure that many of us will reflect many times upon your themes of overcoming fear, respect, trust, preparation and the learnings we have while making the journey to the top.

> Rogers Vaughn, Director
> TEFLON Finishes Worldwide
> Du Pont Polymers

On Meeting the Challenge of Change:

We all believe that your presentation came at just the right time as Shanghai demands to meet the challenges of change on a daily basis. Your integration of leadership and motivation into the dramatic experience of your ascent of Mount Everest has left an important mark in the minds of many people I spoke to after the seminar, and I am sure your presentation will be remembered for a long, long time.

> Hans Koch, President
> Association of International Hoteliers
> Shanghai, China

On Staying Focused:

As a continuous improvement manager, I particularly liked your thoughts on positive dissatisfaction as a key to continuous improvement. I was also struck by your emphasis on getting and staying focused. This concept rings very true for us at Indal where, because of a renewed and strengthened focus over the last few years, we have achieved very positive results. Indeed, during this time we have climbed from a deep valley to attain our first peak in many years. Pat Morrow's *f-8 . . . and be there* was also discussed a great deal in relation to being clearly focused, and I believe it will remain a motivational catchphrase for many people.

> Barry Walters
> Continuous Improvement Manager
> Indal Doors and Windows

On Leadership:

The point that most impressed me was that you, as team leader, did not personally reach the summit. You addressed this in a very matter-of-fact manner as you proceeded with details of the ordeals of the climb. As team leader or manager, we have the responsibility to help others succeed in the overall objective. It is not important that we personally have the success, but that the *team* has the success. By making it possible for others to succeed, [you] still received the credit for obtaining the objective.

My experience with executives from all sorts of different companies is that, in many cases, they have tremendous egos that must be fed. Your example of leadership, self sacrifice and humility is a point that needs to be made and expanded to all the management groups you address.

> Thomas E. Fowler, CLU
> Estate & Business Planning

On Courage and Commitment:

You left us with a lasting impression of the flexibility required to meet the challenge of change in our personal and business lives. Most importantly, you helped demonstrate the courage and commitment necessary to reach our goals in the face of any obstacles.

> R.G. Nader, Vice President—Marketing
> Shell Canada Products Limited

On Contributing to the Team:

I particularly appreciated your insight into the important contribution a team member makes toward the accomplishment of a goal. Your enthusiasm and joy for being part of the process vs. needing to be the one (or two) who actually were to climb the final steps, was sincere and contagious . . . a lesson for us all. Sometimes in our personal pursuit of excellence and attainment of individual goals, we lose sight of the bigger picture—that of the common goal. Thanks for reminding us.

Your message touches lives. It reaches into places that some choose to ignore or are too hurried to consider. I am convinced that you, too, are touched each time you share it—you and Everest are of one spirit.

> Sharil Baxter, Agency Executive
> Blue Cross/Blue Shield of Kansas City

APPENDIX B

One Step Beyond WorldWide Client List

Nobody does it alone. The success that One Step Beyond WorldWide has been able to achieve since 1983 is directly related to the support of more than a thousand corporate and professional organizations in twenty countries worldwide. We are proud to call these organizations clients, but more important, we believe they are also friends.

The following is a select list, designed to profile the diverse nature of people from all walks of life, who have been influenced by the Adventure Attitude philosophies:

*Aetna Life & Casualty
*Air Canada
Alcan Aluminium Limited
*Alexander & Alexander Services Inc.
*American Bankers Association
*American Dental Association
*American Family Insurance Group
American Heart Association

---

* Indicates those clients for whom One Step Beyond WorldWide has included multiple keynote presentations and seminars. A return engagement is an important indicator of a satisfied client.

American Society of Association Executives
Amoco Canada Petroleum Limited
Arthur Andersen & Company
Ascom Timeplex Inc.
Asian Sources Media Group
*Association for Fitness in Business
*AT&T Information Systems
*AT&T Network Systems
Australian Information Industry Association
Australian Life & Casualty Limited
*Banff School of Advanced Management
BASF Agricultural Products Group
Baxter Corporation
*Bell Canada
Bell Communications Research
Bell South Cellular Corporation
*Blue Cross & Blue Shield Association
Boehringer Ingelheim Pharmaceuticals Inc.
*Boy Scouts of Canada
*Campbell Soup Company Limited
*Canadian Home Builders Association
*Canadian Imperial Bank of Commerce
*Century Companies of America
*Ciba-Geigy Canada
*CIGNA Insurance Company
Consumers Distributing Inc.
*Coopers & Lybrand Consulting Group
Deaf & Hard of Hearing Services
Deloitte & Touche
Digital Equipment Corporation
*Dun & Bradstreet
DuPont Teflon Worldwide
Duracell Inc.
Ernst & Young
General Foods
*General Motors of Canada Limited

*Great West Life Assurance Company Limited
*GTE Corporation
*Hallmark Cards
HAVI Group (Far East) LP
Hoffman-La Roche Limited
*Holiday Inn Worldwide
Hong Kong Sports Development Board
*IBM Corporation
IBM World Trade Asia Corporation
*Inacom Corporation
Intel Corporation
International Hoteliers Association of Shanghai
International Road Federation
International SemiTech Microelectronics Inc.
*ITT Hartford Insurance
Landscape Architecture Foundation
*Manufacturers Life Insurance Company
McCaw Cellular Communications Inc.
*Meeting Planners International
Microage Computer Centers Inc.
*Million Dollar Round Table
Monsanto Company
Morgan Stanley Asia Limited
*Motorola Inc.
National Association of Life Underwriters
National Electrical Contractors Association
National Financial
National School Boards Association
National Westminster Bank
National Wholesale Druggists Association
NCR Malaysia Sdn. Bhd.
Newbridge Networks Corporation
*New York Life Insurance Company
New Zealand Insurance (NZI Life)
Norcliffe Thayer Inc.
*Northern Telecom Inc.

Pacific Coast Gas Association
*PetroCanada Inc.
Prudential Assurance Co. (New Zealand) Limited
*Prudential Insurance Company of America
Prudential Preferred Financial Services
*Public Works Canada
*Queen's University Executive Program
*Regent Hotels International
Rhone-Poulenc Agriculture Company
*Royal Bank of Canada
Sarawak Economic Development Corporation
Satellite Television Asian Region (STAR) Limited
Seagate Technologies Inc.
Society of Incentive Travel Executives
*Tektronix Inc.
*Texaco Inc.
*Tourism Canada
Triton Container International Inc.
*Unisys Corporation
*US West Communications
Vickers Inc.
*Walgreens
Whitehall Robins Laboratories
*Young Presidents' Organization

SUGGESTED READING

Throughout this book, I have purposely avoided being too specific about my experiences since I believe the lessons that can be learned from the adventures are more important than the individual events. However, I realize that there will be many who will wish to read more about our Everest climb and the experiences of other great explorers from whom similar lessons can be learned.

Below is a selected list of books that I have enjoyed and which I trust will allow you to continue this journey of discovery.

Beattie, Owen and John Geiger. *Frozen in Time: Unlocking the Secrets of the Franklin Expedition*. Saskatoon: Western Producer Prairie Books, 1987.
An anthropologist investigates the deaths of members of John Franklin's ill-fated 1845–48 expedition, exhuming bodies that had been frozen in permafrost for more than 138 years.

Berton, Pierre. *The Arctic Grail: The Quest for the North West Passage and the North Pole 1818-1909*. Toronto: McClelland and Stewart, 1988.
The complete history of the nineteenth-century quest for the elusive sea route linking the Atlantic and Pacific Oceans, and the quest to be the first to stand at the North Pole.

Daniells, Roy. *Alexander Mackenzie and the North West*. London: Faber and Faber, 1969.
Having traced Mackenzie's journeys of discovery, the author analyzes the significance of this adventurer's contribution to Canada.

Gillman, Peter. *Everest: The Best Writing and Pictures from Seventy Years of Human Endeavor*. Boston: Little Brown and Company, 1993.
A compilation of the best stories and photographs of Everest expeditions published on the 40th anniversary of the first ascent of the mountain in 1953. (It includes Sharon Wood's narrative of her 1986 ascent to the top of the world.)

Herbert, Wally. *The Noose of Laurels: The Discovery of the North Pole*. London: Hodder and Stoughton, 1989.
A fascinating analysis of whether Commander Robert E. Peary could have been the first to reach the North Pole in 1909, a claim that is disputed by some modern experts.

Hobson, Alan. *One Step Beyond: Rediscovering the Adventure Attitude*. Banff, Alberta: Altitude Publishing, 1992.
A book on which I collaborated, which describes the adventures of Laurie Skreslet, John Hughes, Mike Beedell, Sharon Wood and Laurie Dexter, and which articulates the Adventure Attitude.

Holzel, Tom, and Audrey Salkeld. *The Mystery of Mallory and Irvine*. London: Jonathan Cape, 1986.
A fascinating analysis of the possibility that George Mallory and Andrew Irvine reached the peak of Everest in 1924 before they disappeared.

Huntford, Roland. *The Last Place on Earth*. London: Hodder and Stoughton, 1979.
The definitive narrative of the race between Britain's Robert

Falcon Scott and Norway's Roald Amundsen to be the first to reach the South Pole in 1911–12.

Lamb, W. Kaye. *The Journals and Letters of Sir Alexander Mackenzie.* London: Cambridge University Press, 1970.
The definitive book on the life of Sir Alexander Mackenzie and his great journeys of discovery, from Montreal to the Arctic Ocean in 1789 and to the Pacific Ocean in 1793.

Morrow, Patrick. *Beyond Everest: Quest for the Seven Summits.* Camden East, Ontario: Camden House Publishing, 1986.
The first-person narrative of Pat Morrow's Everest climb in 1982 and his subsequent ascents to the top of the highest mountains on each of the earth's seven continents.

Patterson, Bruce. *Canadians on Everest.* Calgary, Alberta: Detselig Enterprises, 1990.
Bruce was the Southam news reporter on our 1982 Everest climb and his book describes our expedition in some detail, together with the experiences of other Canadian expeditions to Everest (in 1986, 1987 and 1988).

Stefansson, Vilhjalmur. *Unsolved Mysteries of the Arctic.* New York: Books for Libraries Press, 1938.
Written by one of the Arctic's greatest adventurers, an analysis of the Franklin tragedy and many other intriguing mysteries from northern exploration.

John Amatt has provided an important addition to books available to guide people in their business and personal lives through these rapidly changing times. It is written with the vision and passion familiar to anyone who has met John, or attended one of his talks. John has learnt a great deal from his experiences, and imparts that learning in a highly readable, stimulating manner. *Straight to the Top and Beyond* will occupy a place of honour on my bookshelves.

—Kingsley Smith
President, Management
Development for Asia Ltd.

By exploring the essence of adventure through his own accomplishments and struggles and by demonstrating how these insights can be employed in dealing with the challenges of everyday life, John Amatt sends a powerful, pertinent message to those who strive earnestly to maintain their bearings in a complex and rapidly changing world.

He will also awaken some of the many who dream blissfully that personal comfort and safety are God-given rights.

—Hans Gmoser
Founder and President
Canadian Mountain Holidays

John Amatt has once again made climbing a mountain seem like a routine chore. The understanding of corporate goals is one thing. Encouraging individuals to shake off their limitations, many of which are self-imposed, will be a challenge for all of us if we are to face up to the speed of change in the 21st Century without fear.

—Howard J.C. Wells
Chief Executive, Hong Kong
Sports Development Board

John Amatt has drawn on his personal odyssey of always reaching for the top to identify nine keys to success in dealing with the challenges of the coming millennium.

—Claude Taylor
Chairman Emeritus
Air Canada